INHALE

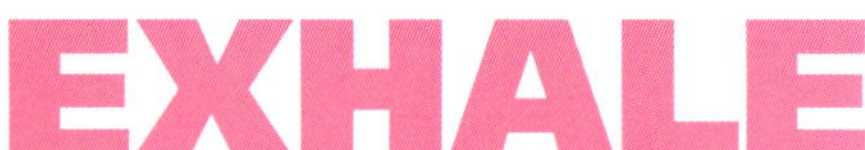

EXHALE

An installation commissioned
to mark the reopening
of Manchester Art Gallery

25 May 2002 - 30 June 2002

Content

Sponsor's Statement

Manchester Airport is delighted to sponsor Michael Craig-Martin's exhibition, Inhale/Exhale. As an artist whose work has been championed largely in Europe and America in recent years, we are particularly proud to be involved in bringing Craig-Martin to Manchester.

This sponsorship, which coincides with one of the most exciting visual arts developments in the region, is a great prospect both for the people of the North West and for the visitors that Manchester Art Gallery will undoubtedly attract.

Manchester Airport is one of the country's foremost arts sponsors, investing 1% of gross profit each year in the arts. A wide and varied award winning programme includes local community projects and festivals, through to prestigious regional concerts, performances, exhibitions and international tours.

A continuing catalyst for arts development, Manchester Airport is keen to sponsor new, untried initiatives, as well as supporting creative excellence in the region's premier venues. By sponsoring Craig-Martin's ambitious and breath-taking installation, we are helping to support the commissioning of new work.

The excellence of the Airport's Arts Programme not only enhances the quality of life of the local population, it also develops Manchester's reputation as one of Europe's leading cultural centres.

We are sure this exhibition will be enormously successful. We also congratulate all involved in the re-opening of this wonderful Gallery, which is an asset to the City and its people.

Cllr. Brian Harrison
Chair of Manchester Airport

This book has been published to accompany the inaugural show in the new main exhibition space at Manchester Art Gallery. Over the past four years the Gallery has been transformed following a £35m expansion scheme designed by Michael Hopkins and Partners which provides two purpose-built exhibition galleries. Manchester Art Gallery is now a flagship venue setting standards for the presentation of visual arts both nationally and internationally.

Having previously worked with Michael Craig-Martin when he selected the South Bank Centre National Touring Exhibition of works on paper, *Drawing the Line* which we showed in 1995, we were delighted when he responded so enthusiastically to our invitation to return to Manchester to create a new work to launch our magnificent new top-lit exhibition gallery. In the last few years Craig-Martin has created increasingly ambitious, multicoloured installations which have responded to their varied architectural settings.

Craig-Martin's extraordinary vision has transformed the white walls into a symphony of colour and line creating a stunning and vivid spectacle. *Inhale/Exhale* is both subtle and complex in its allusions as it questions how we see and perceive the world and the things that surround us. This book documents the making of this installation, exploring the extensive thought process behind it. *Inhale/Exhale* is Craig-Martin's largest painted installation in the UK and his first solo exhibition here since his retrospective at the Whitechapel Art Gallery in 1989.

We would like to thank Richard Cork for his insightful and thought provoking essay which puts *Inhale/Exhale* in the context of Craig-Martin's work of the last thirty years and Virginia Button for her lively and illuminating interview. We would also like to thank Craig-Martin's dedicated assistants, Paul Hosking and Jost Muenster and his additional Manchester assistant, Paul Needham. All three worked tirelessly to achieve his vision. We are also grateful to Mollie Dent-Brocklehurst of Gagosian Gallery for her help. Manchester Airport has a long history of supporting the arts and we are delighted that they have so generously agreed to sponsor this exhibition. We are also grateful to the Henry Moore Foundation and to Malmaison and ICI Dulux for their support. But above all we must extend our thanks to Michael Craig-Martin for creating such a spectacular and exuberant work for Manchester.

Virginia Tandy, Director
Howard Smith, Head of Curatorial Services
Manchester City Galleries

Foreword

Michael Craig-Martin
Inhale/Exhale
25 May - 30 June 2002

A Manchester City Galleries Exhibition
Organised by Tim Wilcox and Natasha Howes
Book concept and design, Chrissie Morgan
© Manchester City Galleries, Michael Craig-Martin,
Richard Cork, Virginia Button

Inhale/Exhale photo credits:
John Davies pp. cover, back cover, 13, 45-48, 50-59
Richard Weltman pp. 26-43, 64
Alan Seabright pp. 49, 64
Other photo credits:
Gautier Deblonde p.7, Simon Wilson p.9, Todd Eberle p.12,
Dave Lambert p.12, Prudence Cuming Associates p.16-17,
Juan García Rosell p.19, Helge Mundt p.19,
Gary and Tanja Duszynski p.20, John Kellet p.20
Images pp.26-43 scanned by Colourpoint Ltd, Manchester

Printed by Richard Edward Printers, London
Book typeset using Humanist 777
Printed on 170g/m^2 Parilux Silk

Manchester Art Gallery
Mosley Street
Manchester, M2 3JL
T +44 (0) 161 235 8888
F +44 (0) 161 235 8899
www.manchestergalleries.org

Exhibition sponsored by Manchester Airport

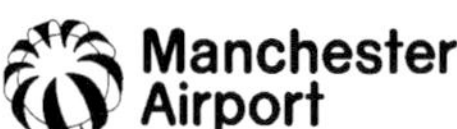

Supported by The Henry Moore Foundation

ISBN 0 901673 56 0
Cover and back cover image:
2nd Floor Exhibition Gallery, Manchester Art Gallery

Images on pp 43: *Students from an after school art club from
Whalley Range 11-18 High School visiting the installation*

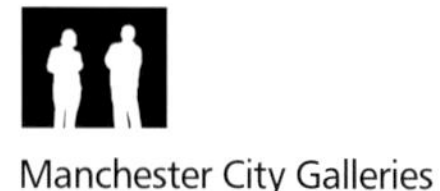

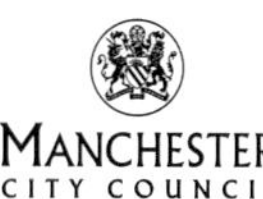

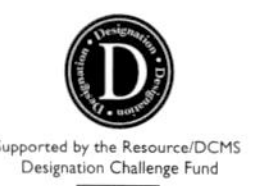

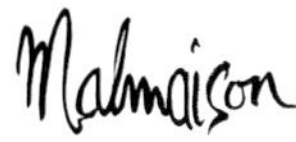

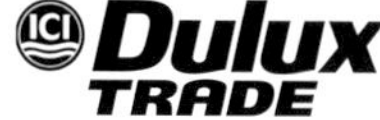

Richard Cork

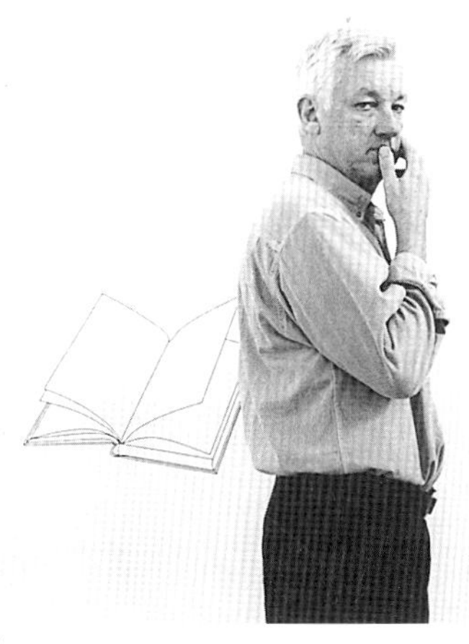

1

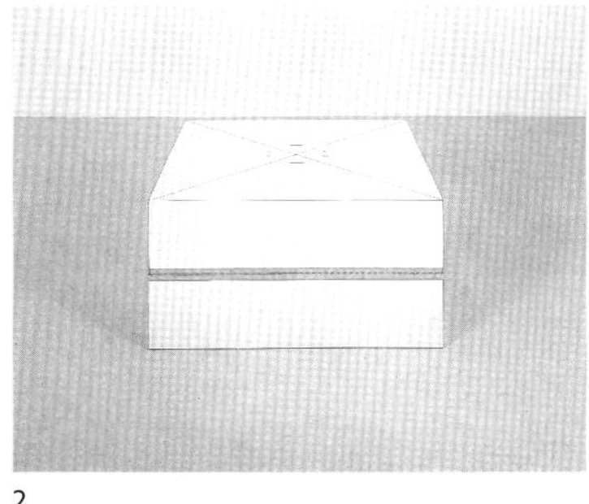

2

3

Nothing, on the face of it, could appear more matter-of-fact or familiar than the objects so limpidly presented in Michael Craig-Martin's work. From the outset of his career he favoured seemingly simple forms, often redolent of domestic use. The boxes in the late 1960s, made with materials as ordinary as formica, plywood and blockboard, looked as if they might have a definable household purpose. But once opened up, they turned out to frustrate conventional expectations. Folded outwards, *Formica Box* (2) ceased to be a container: laid flat on the floor, the pallid structure underwent a mystifying metamorphosis and defied all attempts to pin its function down. *Long Box* (3) became equally enigmatic, despite the deceptive simplicity of its painted, hinged components. As for *Progression of Five Boxes with Lids Reversed* (4,p.8), they unsettled us by refusing to be saddled with a practical role of any kind. Halfway between the condition of vessels and cradles, they invited our inspection and then, without warning, made us realise how unknowable they really were.

At the centre of Craig-Martin's work, then, we are confronted by a fascinating and inexhaustible paradox. The clarity of his making tempts us to imagine that he is essentially a straightforward artist, who wants to beguile as wide an audience as possible with enticing, immediate and accessible images. But as soon as we accept his invitation to contemplate and explore, he makes us conscious of the instability endemic in the world of visible appearances. The most unassuming object turns into a form of infinite ambiguity. The longer we look at it, the more insecure its true identity grows. The four buckets placed in the corners of *On the Table's* wooden surface may seem orderly enough (5,p.8). But the 'table' is unsupported by legs of any kind, and hovers in space with the help of slender nylon ropes attached to the ceiling. Although the water in the buckets plays a crucial part in their effort to remain steady, we are aware that the entire assemblage could lose its composure and collapse, spilling liquid, on the ground below.

Everywhere you look in Craig-Martin's *oeuvre*, the sense of precariousness is inescapable. The milk-bottles in *On the Shelf* (6,p.8) tilt downwards at an alarming angle. Even if their imbalance is rectified, in the line made by the surface of water running through all the bottles, they still look vulnerable. Nor does Craig-Martin concern himself solely with uncertainty in material terms. As the 1970s proceeded, he placed the onlooker's psychological reaction at the forefront of his work. With the aid of eleven vertical strips of mirror, tape and handwriting inscribed directly on the gallery wall, he turned *Society* (8,p.9) into an increasingly uneasy meditation on the notion of self-image and how others might see us. Each viewer, obliged to peer closely at every small mirror and the even more diminutive words written beneath, was made aware of the

1
Michael Craig-Martin
Photo: Gautier Deblonde

2
Formica Box 1968 (remade in 1989)
Formica on plywood
The artist, courtesy of Gagosian Gallery

3
Long Box 1969 (remade in 1989)
Painted plywood
The artist, courtesy of Gagosian Gallery

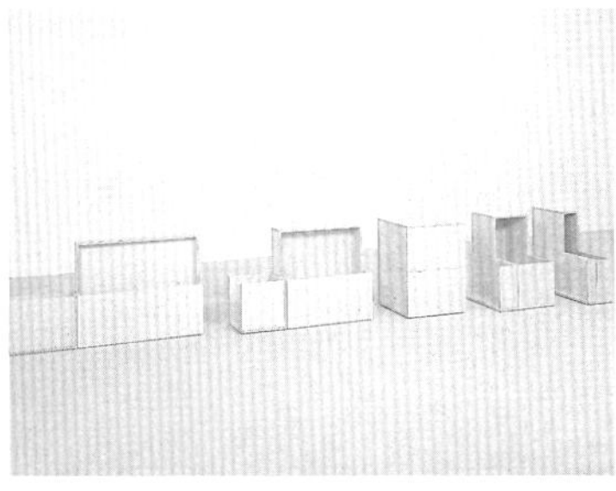

4

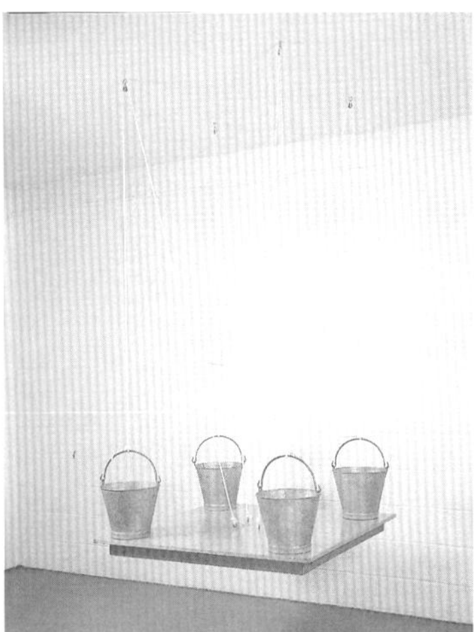

5

disparity between the 'idea of what I am like' and the 'idea of how I appear to others'. Succeeding mirrors combined with their captions to explore the gap separating a conscious social persona from its other, more unfathomable side. Acknowledging that 'part of what I intend others miss', the words went on to admit an even greater complexity: 'part of what I don't recognise others see'. We were left with a mystery, and our gathering realisation of how much lay beyond comprehension altered our response to the reflection in the mirror. On one level the face gazing out from the glass never changed; and yet our perception of these familiar features subtly shifted every time we reappraised them.

The climax of this development arrived with *An Oak Tree* (colour plate 1, p.17), where Craig-Martin confined himself to placing a plain glass of water on the kind of glass shelf usually associated with a bathroom cabinet. Positioned high and alone on an otherwise empty wall, it could not be reached by anyone eager to sample the water or dislodge the entire clinical ensemble. Nevertheless, *An Oak Tree* soon became notorious, deliberately exemplifying some of the most contentious and provocative aspects of conceptual art. For Craig-Martin made clear, in an accompanying text where he conducted an interview with himself, that the glass had undergone a startling metamorphosis. Asked to describe the work, he explained that 'what I've done is change a glass of water into a full-grown oak tree without altering the accidents of the glass of water'. During the course of the interview, Craig-Martin fielded an increasingly aggressive series of questions. He used the sceptical persona of the interviewer to voice the objections raised by many commentators who attacked and vilified the work. But the persona of the artist stayed resolute and unapologetic. When the impatient interviewer asked him 'isn't this just a case of the emperor's new clothes?', his response was firm: 'No. With the emperor's new clothes people claimed to see something which wasn't there because they felt they should. I would be very surprised if anyone told me they saw an oak tree'.

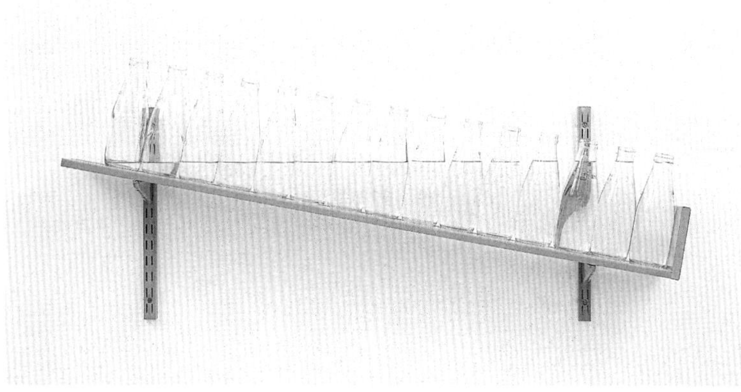

6

7
Faces 1972
Installation in *7 Exhibitions*,
Tate Gallery, London
Photo: Simon Wilson

8
Society 1973
Mirror, tape and handwriting on wall
The artist, courtesy of Gagosian Gallery

9
Modern Dance 1981
Tape on wall, variable dimensions, size
determined at each installation
The artist, courtesy of Gagosian Gallery

By relying on such a commonsensical, eminently reasonable approach to the conundrum he had set up, Craig-Martin revealed the vein of disarming adroitness that accompanied even his most subversive strategies. Like Marcel Duchamp, who did so much to inaugurate the seminal shift in focus away from the object towards the artist's own intentions, he knew how to deploy a witty and seductive form of cunning. The aplomb of a conjuror was evoked in a 1975 neon piece entitled *Sleight-of-Hand* (colour plate 2, p.18), where the anonymous performer's out-stretched fingers shifted with each flash of the blue-white tubes. The gesture conveyed the classic moment of disclosure, when the magician reveals the full extent of his trickery by showing that his hand is empty. Craig-Martin seeks a similar relationship with his viewers, drawing them into an engagement with the work by relying on an almost theatrical display of deftness and mischievous humour.

Towards the close of the 1970s, he stopped relying on such a wide array of materials and ways of working. The buckets, boxes, clipboards, paint tins, bottles and mirrors gave way to a more single-minded involvement with tape, using it is a linear device capable of producing wall-drawings on a titanic scale. Their monumental dimensions did not, however, make them at all ponderous. Ease and lightness were their hallmarks. Even an object as substantial as a hammer was limited to contours alone, and they flowed effortlessly into the purged outlines of a sandal and a sardine can, its lid rolled back to disclose the void within. Implicit in Craig-Martin's choice of still life was a democratic belief that the most quotidian forms deserved to be invested with dignity. But there was nothing grandiose about their stripped, austere poise. Floating on the wall with unforced serenity, these strangely weightless denizens of Craig-Martin's universe delighted in an almost balletic *élan*. He took risks in many of his colossal drawings, as the objects interweaved and overlapped with a complexity that could easily have grown congested. His innate sense of clarity prevented them from becoming tortuous, though. Drawn with the rigorous simplicity of a diagram, they described exuberant arcs and loops in space that never ended up destroying the forms' ability to be recognised.

Initially, Craig-Martin restricted the wall-drawings to black tape. But by the time he executed *Modern Dance* (9) in 1981, red was introduced as well to pick out the contours of the four objects floating at the front of the ensemble: a tin-opener, an upside-down gun, a pair of spectacles and a safety-pin. As its title promised, *Modern Dance* added up to an energising display. The forms glided and tumbled with the fluidity of utensils in a space-rocket, liberated from gravitational constraints as they abandoned their moorings and floated free. Behind them, outlined in black, a stepladder, book, globe and coat were ranged in a coolly

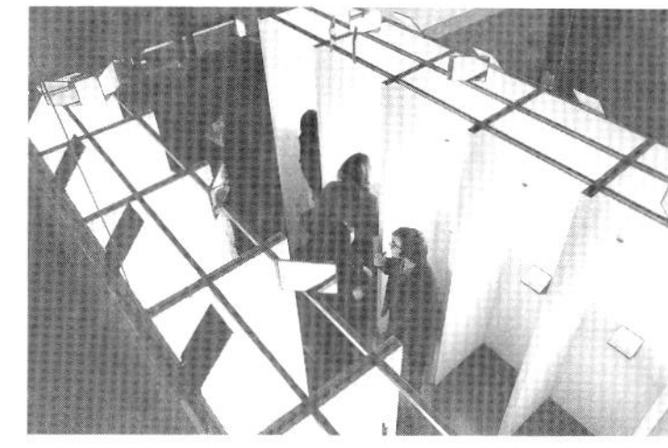

7

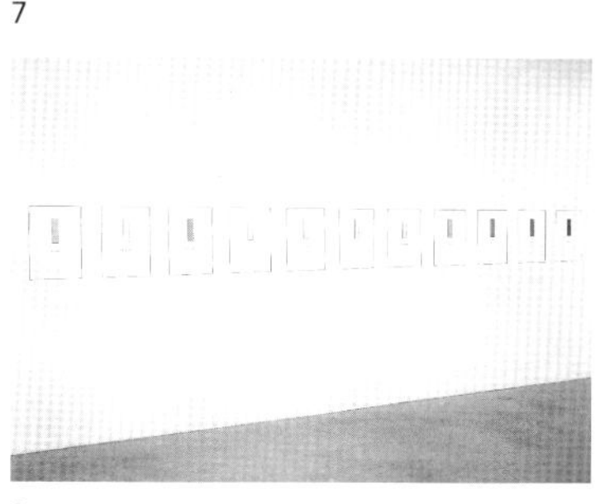

8

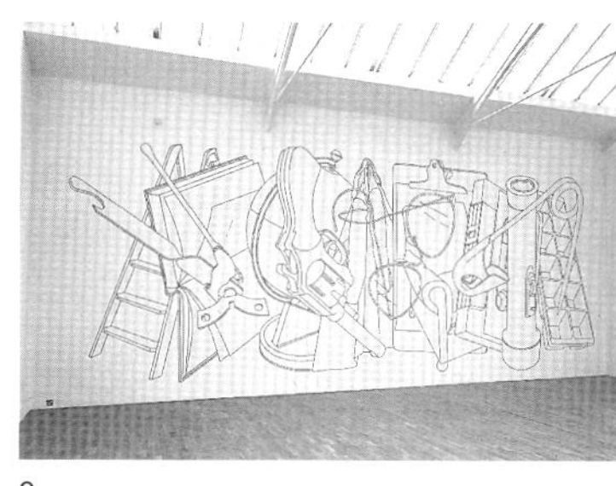

9

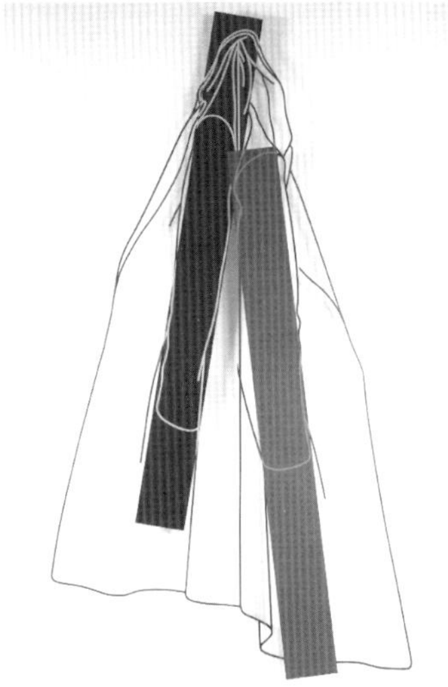

10

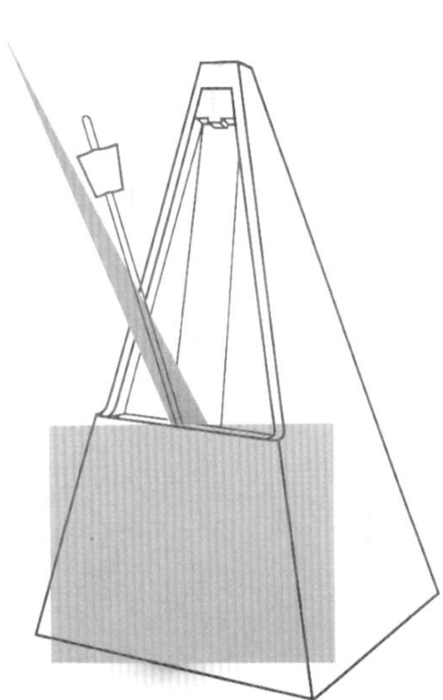

11

organised frieze with a clipboard, tape-recorder, torch and ice-tray. Although some of them were overtly modern appliances, there was no suspicion of straining after contemporaneity in an awkward or programmatic way. Rather did Craig-Martin make them seem inevitable, and the rigorous neo-classicism of his drawing style helped to lend them an air of satisfying finality.

The assurance with which Craig-Martin commanded large-scale surfaces meant that he was well-equipped to tackle architectural settings. The first time I came across the outcome of such a commission was in 1984, when he produced a big untitled wall-drawing for the Blackwater floor of Colchester General Hospital. He achieved an impressive alliance between image and wall, with a graceful linear interweaving of everyday objects that gave the adjacent children's wards a spirited sense of well-being. Even here, however, hints of darker emotions could be detected within the prevailing mood of euphoria. An inverted umbrella lay in one corner of the image. Surmounted by a predatory fork, it looked inexplicably discarded and forlorn.

Signs of tension were also detectable within other, ostensibly tranquil works of the same period. In *Man* (10), the outlines of a coat hanging from the wall were disrupted by two aluminium panels, one painted black and the other grey. Their tautness had a disturbing force, quite at variance with the placidity of the coat's capacious folds. And a similar element of sharpness was inserted into *Metronome* (11) the following year, where the black steel rods defining the instrument were contrasted with painted aluminium panels of light blue and scarlet. At first, they appeared to enliven the starkness of the metronome, but the scarlet form sliced through space like a dagger. Echoing the hand of the metronome, it suggested that Craig-Martin's attitude towards the ever-ticking progress of time was, at best, highly ambivalent.

Not all these insertions seemed so ominous. In *Side-Step* (12), a framed fragment of a real aluminium ladder was lodged within a steel-rod 'drawing' of the same appliance. The effect was undoubtedly surprising, but far from sinister. It made the viewer think about different ways of dealing with an object, as well as Craig-Martin's fascination with the dialogue between reality and its representation through art.
In *Globe* (13), on the other hand, the insertion of a deep blue painted wood cube was more disconcerting. It appeared to engulf the globe, suggesting that the entire spinning world had somehow become trapped and solidified within this protruding alien slab.

The globe appeared still more threatened in an ample 1989 painting, where most of the picture-surface was flooded by unalleviated

10
Man 1984
Oil on aluminium panels with painted steel rods
Ferens Art Gallery, Hull Museums and Art Galleries

11
Metronome 1985
Oil on aluminium panels with painted steel rods
Jacobson Townsley & Co.

12
Side-Step 1987
Aluminium and painted steel rods with
aluminium ladder
Private collection

13
Globe 1986
Oil on wood with painted steel rods
Private collection

blackness. Only a modest white oblong resisted the nocturnal expanse, and the globe's outlines were clearly asserted there. But it could have been overwhelmed at any instant by the dark beyond; and in a far larger canvas painted the same year, a light bulb was reduced to a still smaller rectangle of whiteness surrounded by inky immensity. The mood of apprehensiveness was impossible to overlook.

In most of his work, Craig-Martin avoids any direct reference to the human figure. Even when a jacketed man was placed at the very centre of *Still Life with Interior* (14,p.12), the title did not acknowledge his presence. Deprived of a head, he remained anonymous. And the segments of ladder flanking him on both sides looked oddly disjointed, implying that access to this enigmatic individual was barred. That is why the inclusion of a human skeleton in an untitled painting thirteen years later was so remarkable. Clearly a figure of Death, he extended his bony hand towards an outsized scythe that curved round him before terminating, with undisguised symbolism, in front of a metronome. Mortality and transience were perhaps to be expected in a canvas executed during the millennium year of 2000. But this grim presence still has the ability to unsettle, and alerts us to the possibility that disquieting elements may also be found in the prodigious installation Craig-Martin has now produced for the reopening of Manchester Art Gallery.

The primary mood of this overwhelming and exclamatory work, which refuses to be daunted by the vastness of the room it enlivens, is positive. As befits the inauguration of Michael Hopkins' major new extension, *Inhale/Exhale* has been carried out with irresistible panache. Craig-Martin's previous experience of tackling architectural interiors as diverse as the Centre del Carme in Valencia (colour plate 3, p.19), the Kunstverein in Hanover (colour plate 4, p.19) and the Museum of Modern Art in New York (15, p.12) has given him a formidable amount of assurance when dealing with monumental spaces. Far from unnerving him, the challenge presented by each new commission seems to stimulate Craig-Martin and encourage him to become ever more audacious. I remember being particularly impressed by his approach to the MoMA rooms, which many artists would have found frankly inhibiting. With an air of absolute confidence, he even managed to create a felicitous new context for modernist icons as familiar as De Chirico's *The Song of Love*, Duchamp's *Bicycle Wheel* and Picasso's seminal Cubist *Guitar*. At the same time, Craig-Martin succeeded in proclaiming his own identity with images ranging in mood from a tall, menacing angle-poise lamp to a modest yet delectable cluster of blue bananas. Treading a tightrope between the twin pitfalls of deference and over-assertiveness, he maintained his balance in even the most hallowed art-historical surroundings.

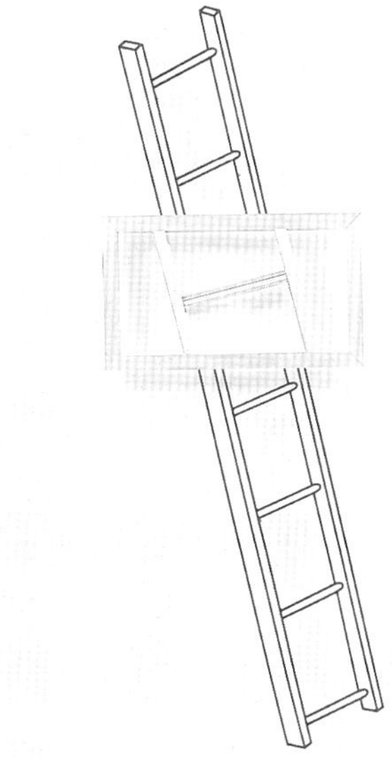

12

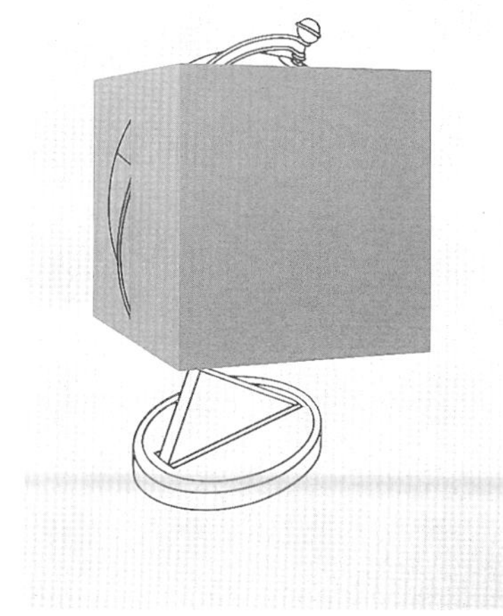

13

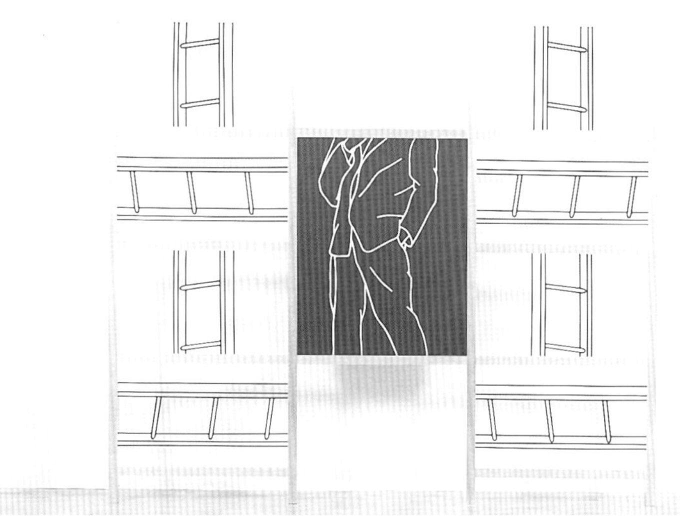

14

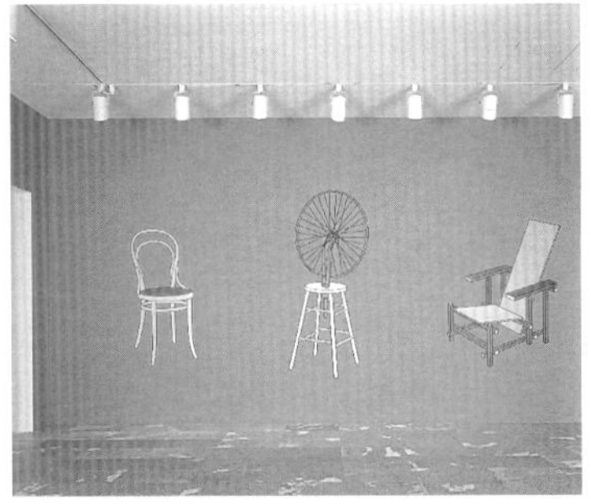

15

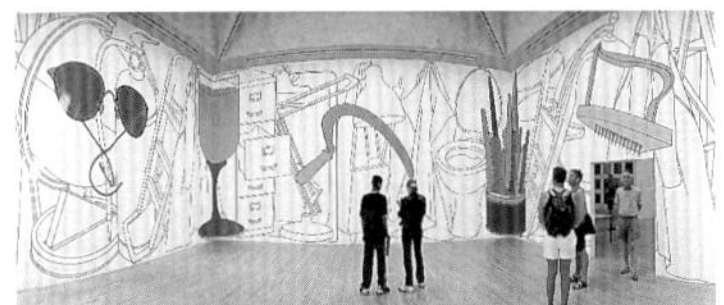

16

Although the room at Manchester is a colossal 420 square metres, larger by far than the grand painted installation Craig-Martin executed for Tate Britain's *Intelligence: New British Art 2000* (16), he has handled it with characteristic lucidity and aplomb. As I approached the left doorway from the top-floor landing of Hopkins' new wing, a titanic pink light-bulb appeared to be suspended on the far wall. Tilting at a slightly jaunty angle, it seemed to hold out a promise of great pictorial playfulness, of luminosity and dancing emancipation. Nor was I disappointed when, on the other side of the doorway, the entire panoramic width of the wall opened up in front of me. Saturated in magenta, this spectacular expanse has been transformed into one of the most harmonious, subtly nuanced compositions Craig-Martin has ever produced. The light bulb turns out to be flanking a central image of a canvas-back. Its pale blue surface is also reminiscent of a blithe sky in high summer, suggesting that we are looking through a window. But fragments of a globe are detectable behind, effectively destroying the window illusion and introducing, at the same time, a more teasing notion of objects largely hidden from view.

Not that the rest of the wall appears to be withholding pictorial information. The metronome, flanking the canvas on the other side and thereby acting as a complement to the light bulb, is defined with all the lucidity at Craig-Martin's command. So is the tape-cassette beside it, even if the lowest corner has been cut off by the floor. The slicing implies that the forms on this wall are able to travel beyond the room's physical limits - an idea confirmed by some of the objects above,

17-18
Inhale/Exhale (details) 2002
Installation at Manchester Art Gallery
Photo: John Davies

partially disappearing into the ceiling. Although Craig-Martin could not have been more attentive to the character of the architectural space at his disposal, he also feels at liberty to challenge its boundaries with hints of an unseen world beyond.

All the same, he decided not to implement his original plan and let the two chairs, placed at the outer edges of the composition, travel right up to the ceiling. They now terminate lower down and, like most of the forms on this wall, remain intact. Moreover, they occupy a space quickened by a considerable amount of spatial recession. The filing-cabinet and stepladder, positioned behind the light-bulb and metronome respectively, seem relegated to the far distance. Craig-Martin initially intended them to be larger, but once he started work on the installation *in situ* they were both considerably reduced. As a result, the entire wall is enlivened by a greater degree of scale contrasts, along with the push and pull of objects that dive back or press themselves insistently upon us.

The wonder is that they stop well short of disrupting the composition's overall poise and serenity. We soon become aware of the reciprocity between the book (17) on one side and the tape-cassette (18) on the other. It makes us realise, in the deftest manner imaginable, of the balancing references Craig-Martin sets up here between music and literature, sound and words. A similar dialogue is established by pairing the jumbo-sized sardine tin, its lid rolled back to disclose a puce interior, with the ice-tray. Both objects thrust down at arresting diagonals from different sides of the wall, embodying the distinct yet related attractions of water and food, drinking and eating.

Although no people are discernible here, everything seems suffused with human associations. The fire extinguisher and pencil sharpener, standing like mute sentinels at either end of the far wall, seem eager to be picked up and put to good use. So do the objects floating on the two side walls, filling our peripheral vision when we stand in the middle of the room. The television set, defiantly unaltered in design ever since Craig-Martin first drew it during the 1970s, is waiting to be switched on. And its equivalent on the other side, a dark green metal drawer, demands to be filled with documents. The trolley near the TV is ready to be stacked with cargo and pushed to a new destination; while the lavatory on the opposite side, so much smaller than the drawer that we wonder precisely what spatial position it occupies, sits with lid raised expectantly. Then there are the chairs, one resolutely old-fashioned and the other proud of its classic modernist simplicity. They both seem to be preparing themselves for the weight of anyone wanting to rest on their welcoming seats.

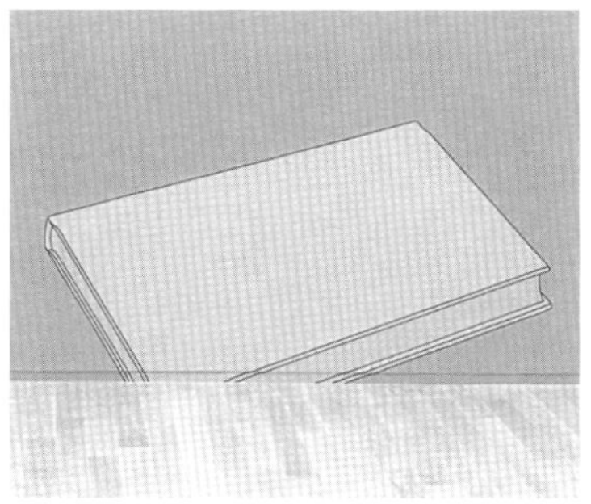

17

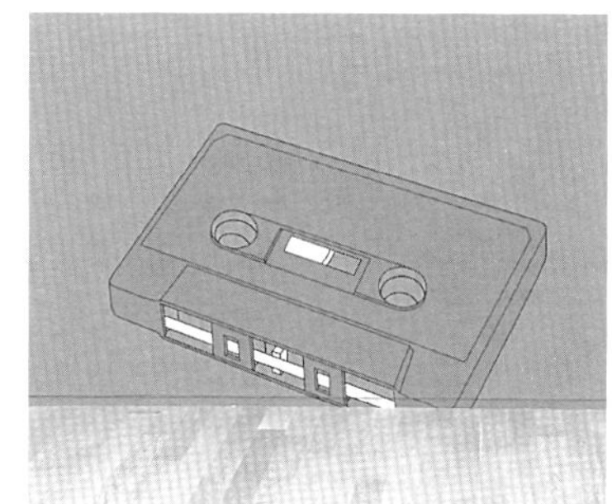

18

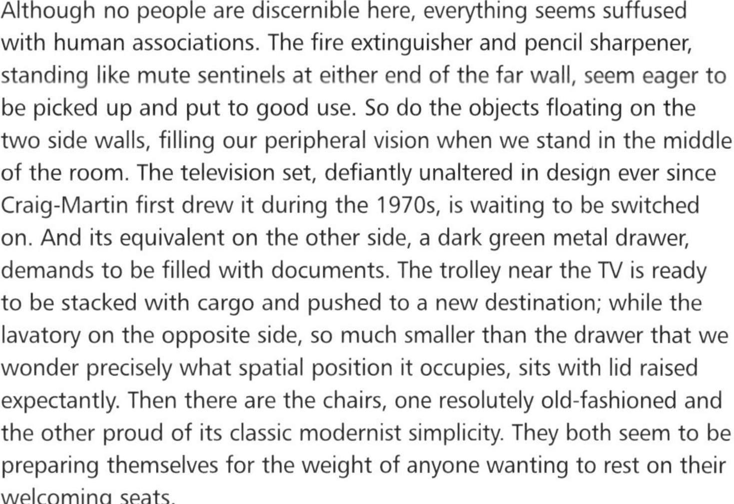

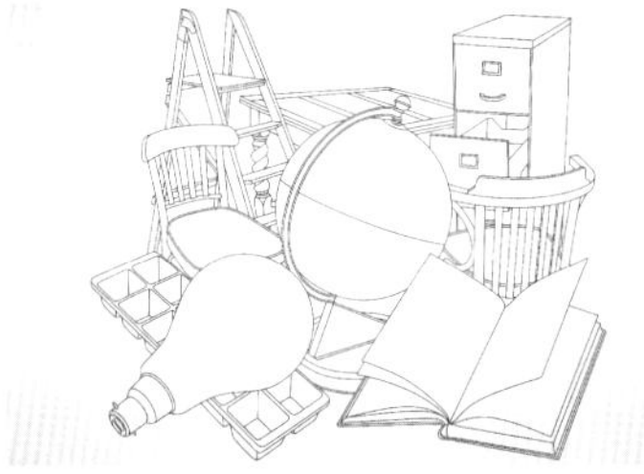

19

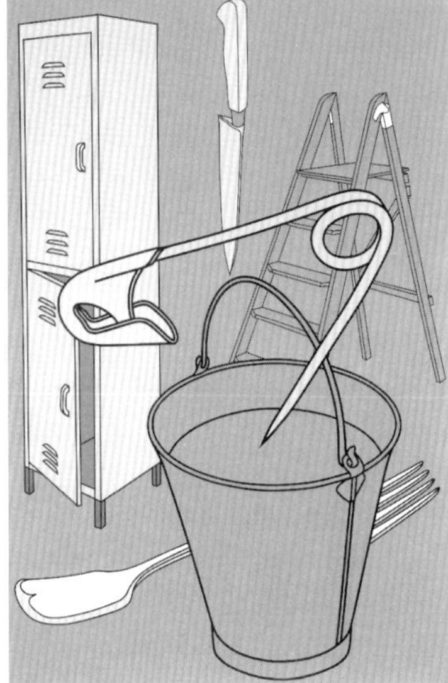

20

Alongside their willingness to fulfil a particular function, however, the forms in Craig-Martin's work also look disconcertingly empty. The lid of the sardine tin has been peeled back to disclose nothing within. The ice-tray appears just as vacant, and the filing-cabinet next to it has a pulled-out, vacant drawer at its centre. Although the television set may be switched on, the screen is filled with a mysterious, uninformative redness. Moreover, the stepladder stands idle, bereft of any sign of usage by its owner. Everything on these walls appears strangely becalmed, almost to the point of seeming paralysed. Craig-Martin's decision to leave both side-walls bare beyond the two chairs, adds to this sense of frozen solitude. Aside from the canvas propped so surprisingly against the globe, nothing touches anything else. No object is allowed to invade its neighbour, and this stillness makes the near blotting-out of the globe seem even more intriguing. Why should the world itself be largely hidden, by a canvas that refuses to disclose what might have been painted on its front, unseen surface?

In the main, though, Craig-Martin sustains a nourishing tension between isolation on the one hand and a potential sense of community on the other. It gives these painted walls their central fascination, and prompts us to wonder about the strangeness inherent in a gathering of things that appeared, at first glance, so untroubled.

The mystery intensifies still further as soon as we swing round and look at the opposite wall. For here Craig-Martin has limited himself to colouring the space between the doors lime-green, and hanging a single canvas executed in his London studio. In this rigorously calculated painting, the objects floating on the walls are reassembled as a tight-packed yet magisterial still life. Since the entire installation is called Inhale/Exhale, he surely wants us to imagine that the forms have somehow been sucked from the walls into the more compact limits of this easel painting. At any rate, there they all are. Some can undoubtedly be seen better than before. Freed from its humiliating position behind the canvas back, the globe now occupies the centre of the stage. The yellow chair in front enjoys a far more prominent space than it did on the wall, and the pencil-sharpener has been transformed into an imposing foreground monolith. Everything is now clustered together, in a composition notable for a sense of *horror vacui*. Glimpses of the walls' magenta ground can still be seen in the lower corners of the painting, and another fragment is visible at the top. On the whole, however, the objects cram the picture-space to bursting-point.

As a result, the image could hardly be further removed from the free-flowing harmony of the walls. Craig-Martin's sudden changes of

19
Reading (with Globe) 1980
Tape on wall, variable dimensions, size determined at each installation
The Trustees of the Tate Gallery, London

20
Pricks 2000
Acrylic on canvas
The artist, courtesy of Gagosian Gallery

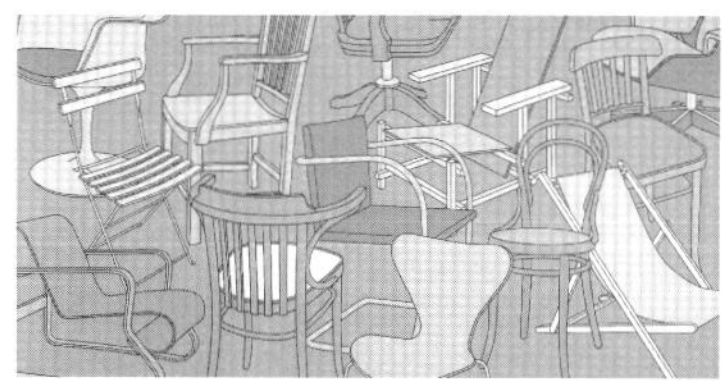

21

21
California Dreaming 2001
Acrylic on canvas
The artist, courtesy
of Gagosian Gallery

Colour Plates pp. 16-20

1
An Oak Tree 1973
Metal, glass, water
Australian National Gallery, Canberra
Photo: Prudence Cuming Associates

2
Sleight-of-hand 1975
Neon
The artist, courtesy of Gagosian Gallery

3
Installation 2000 at IVAM, Centre del
Carme, Valencia
Photo: Juan García Rosell
Courtesy Photographic Archive, IVAM,
Generalitat Valencia

4
Always Now 1998
Installation at Kunstverein, Hannover
Photo: Helge Mundt, courtesy Kunstverein
Hannover

5
and sometimes a cigar is just a cigar 1999
Württembuergischer Kunstverein, Stuttgart
Photo: Gary and Tanja Duszynski

6
Landscapes 2001
Installation Douglas Hyde Gallery, Dublin
Photo: John Kellet

scale seem all the more provocative in this densely organised storage
chamber. Why is the book so much smaller than the sardine tin? How
come the single drawer, relegated now to the background, dominates
the filing-cabinet in front of it? The fire-extinguisher appears oddly
minuscule up against the TV set and the size of the gigantic light bulb
seems out of all proportion to the globe.

Even more curious is the absence of any map on the globe's grey
surface. It remains as blank as the television screen, and nothing can
now be seen in its entirety. Far more of the globe may be visible, but it
is still interrupted by the yellow chair and, to a greater extent, the
metronome with its hand arrested in the same position as before. The
trolley has been sliced off by the base of the canvas, while the tape-
cassette is now perched rather precariously on the ice-tray's open
compartments. Everything overlaps, in a packed and powerfully
claustrophobic image quite unlike most of Craig-Martin's earlier still-life
paintings. Their contents never used to impinge on each other, whereas
here they seem pushed together and trapped in a space so confined
that we long, after a while, to set them free.

That is why *Inhale/Exhale* is such an exhilarating work to encounter and
explore. Stimulated by the title, we find ourselves fantasizing about the
painting's ability to breathe out as well as in. Its component parts could
equally well be blown out of the canvas and back onto the wall.
Turning from one side of the room at Manchester to the other, we feel
a palpable sense of release. For the objects on the three walls have
room to expand there, rejoicing in their newly recovered wholeness.

Apart, of course, from the globe, once again almost obscured. The
blocking presence of the canvas back, lodged so imperiously at the
centre of the wall, now seems far more insistent than before. It reflects
a need to make the canvas fulfil its classic role as a window on the
world, acting like a magnet to gather all the objects together and
reassemble them on its surface. Recognising this imperative, Craig-
Martin implies that painters feel driven to impose their own sense of
order. And to a certain extent, he counts himself among these inveterate
picture makers. But as an artist who moves so supply from permanent
paintings in his studio to temporary installations elsewhere, he must
also feel torn between the rival demands of the canvas and the walls,
between a highly refined image and a more freewheeling version of
reality. By dramatising this fundamental conflict in such an epic arena,
Inhale/Exhale displays his open-minded zestfulness as a pictorial juggler,
who never tires of discovering different ways to charge everyday life
with the transforming power of art.

Q: To begin with, could you describe this work?

A: Yes, of course. What I've done is change a glass of water into a
    full-grown oak tree without altering the accidents of the glass
    of water.

Q: The accidents?

A: Yes. The colour, feel, weight, size ...

Q: Do you mean that the glass of water is a symbol of an oak tree?

A: No. It's not a symbol. I've changed the physical substance of the
    glass of water into that of an oak tree.

Q: It looks like a glass of water...

A: Of course it does. I didn't change its appearance. But it's not a
    glass of water. It's an oak tree.

Q: Can you prove what you claim to have done?

A: Well, yes and no. I claim to have maintained the physical form
    of the glass of water and, as you can see, I have. However, as
    one normally looks for evidence of physical change in terms of
    altered form, no such proof exists.

Q: Haven't you simply called this glass of water an oak tree?

A: Absolutely not. It is not a glass of water any more. I have
    changed its actual substance. It would no longer be accurate to
    call it a glass of water. One could call it anything one wished
    but that would not alter the fact that it is an oak tree.

Q: Isn't this just a case of the emperor's new clothes?

A: No. With the emperor's new clothes people claimed to see
    something that wasn't there because they felt they should.
    I would be very surprised if anyone told me they saw an oak tree.

Q: Was is difficult to effect the change?

A: No effort at all. But it took me years of work before I realised
    I could do it.

Q: When precisely did the glass of water become an oak tree?

A: When I put water in the glass.

Q: Does this happen every time you fill a glass with water?

A: No, of course not. Only when I intend to change it into an oak tree.

Q: Then intention causes the change?

A: I would say it precipitates the change.

Q: You don't know how you do it?

A: It contradicts what I feel I know about cause and effect.

Q: It seems to me you're claiming to have worked a miracle. Isn't that the case?

A: I'm flattered that you think so.

Q: But aren't you the only person who can do something like this?

A: How could I know?

Q: Could you teach others to do it?

A: No. It's not something one can teach.

Q: Do you consider that changing the glass of water into an oak
    tree constitutes an artwork?

A: Yes.

Q: What precisely is the artwork? The glass of water?

A: There is no glass of water any more.

Q: The process of change?

A: There is no process involved in the change.

Q: The oak tree?

A: Yes. The oak tree.

Q: But the oak tree only exists in the mind.

A: No. The actual oak tree is physically present but in the form of the
    glass of water. As the glass of water was a particular glass of water,
    the oak tree is also particular. To conceive the category 'oak tree' or to
    picture a particular oak tree is not to understand and experience what
    appears to be a glass of water as an oak tree. Just as it is imperceivable,
    it is also inconceivable.

Q: Did the particular oak tree exist somewhere else before it took
    the form of the glass of water?

A: No. This particular oak tree did not exist previously. I should
    also point out that it does not and will not ever have any other
    form but that of a glass of water.

Q: How long will it continue to be an oak tree?

A: Until I change it.

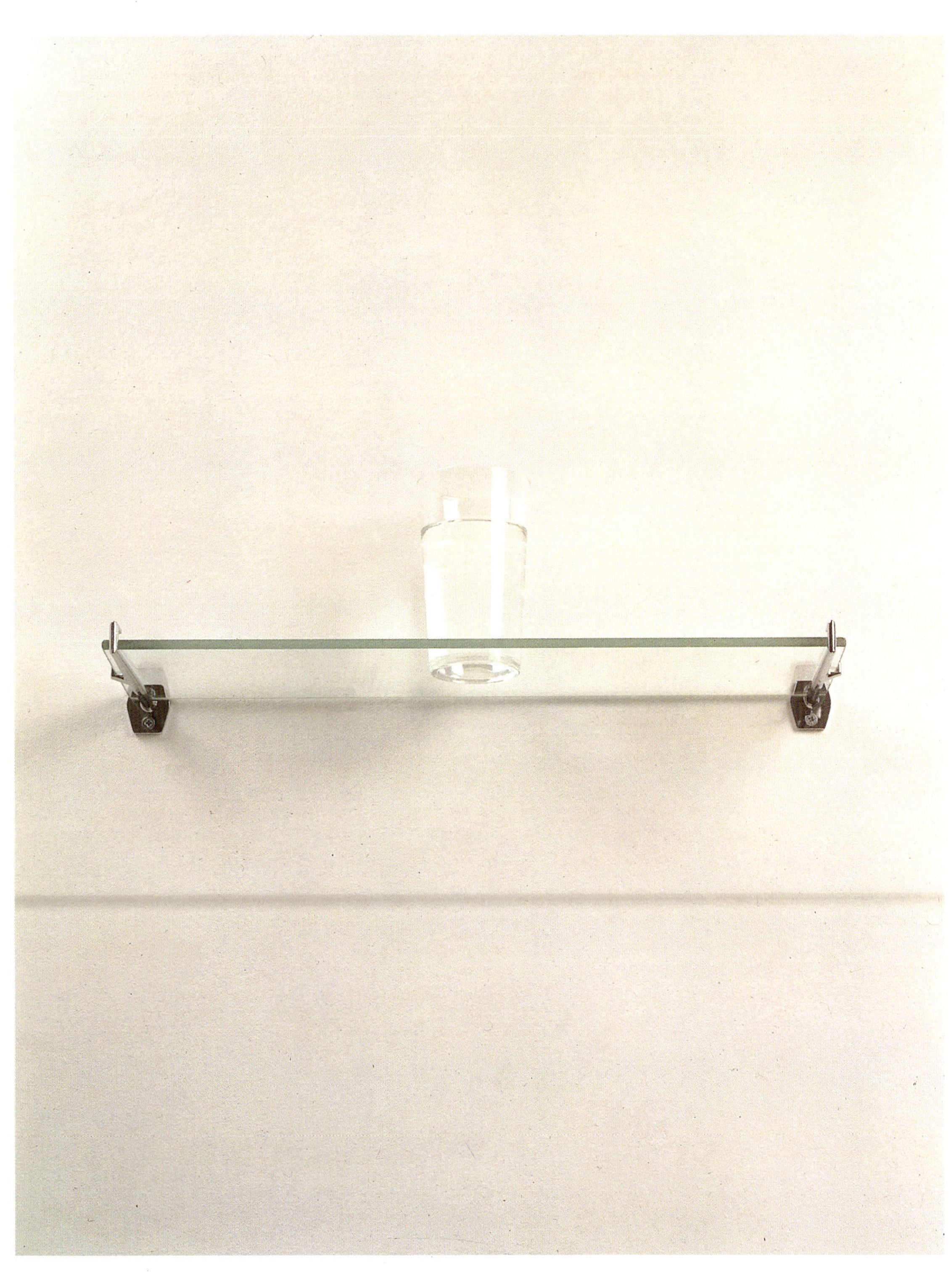

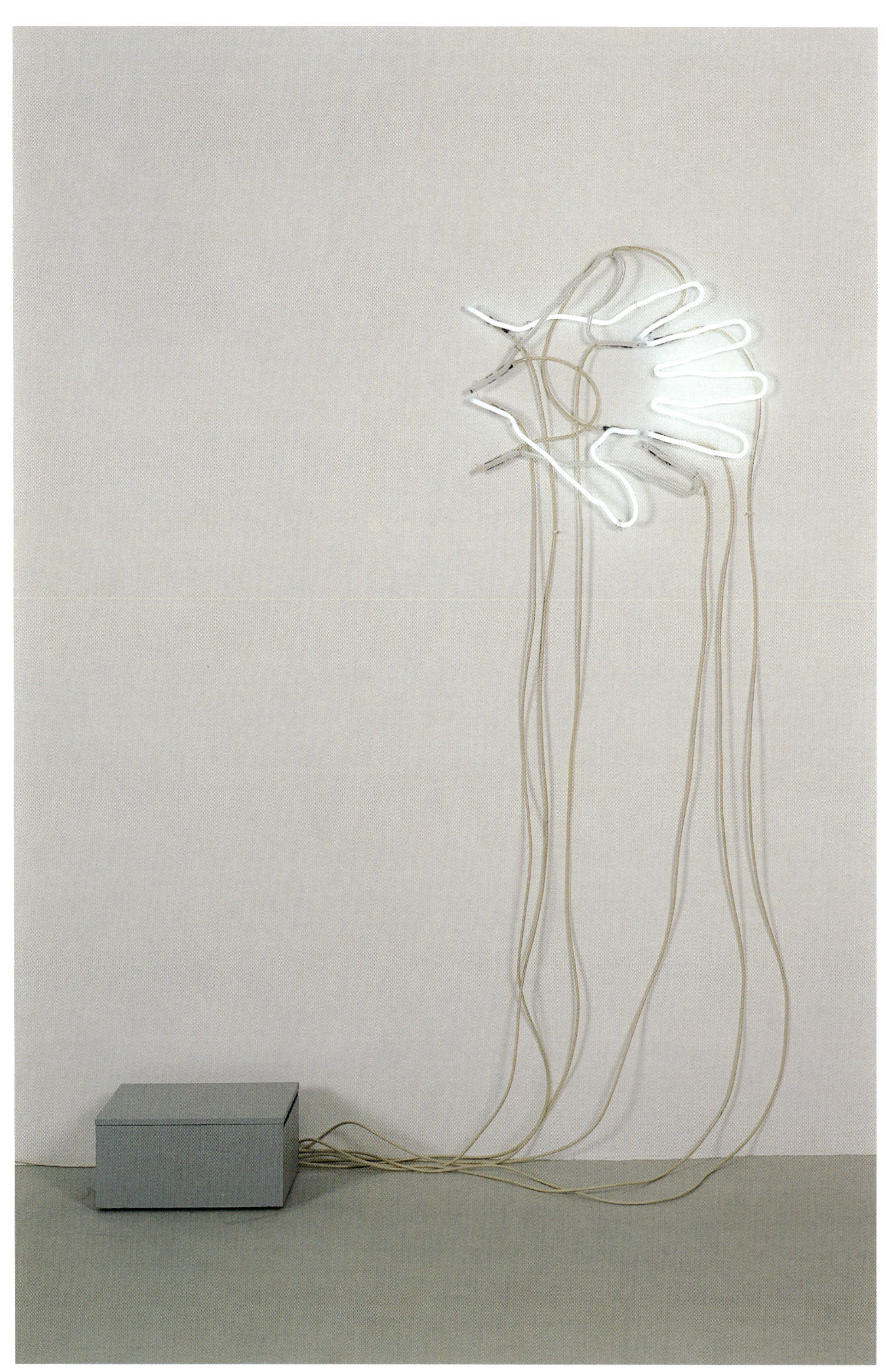

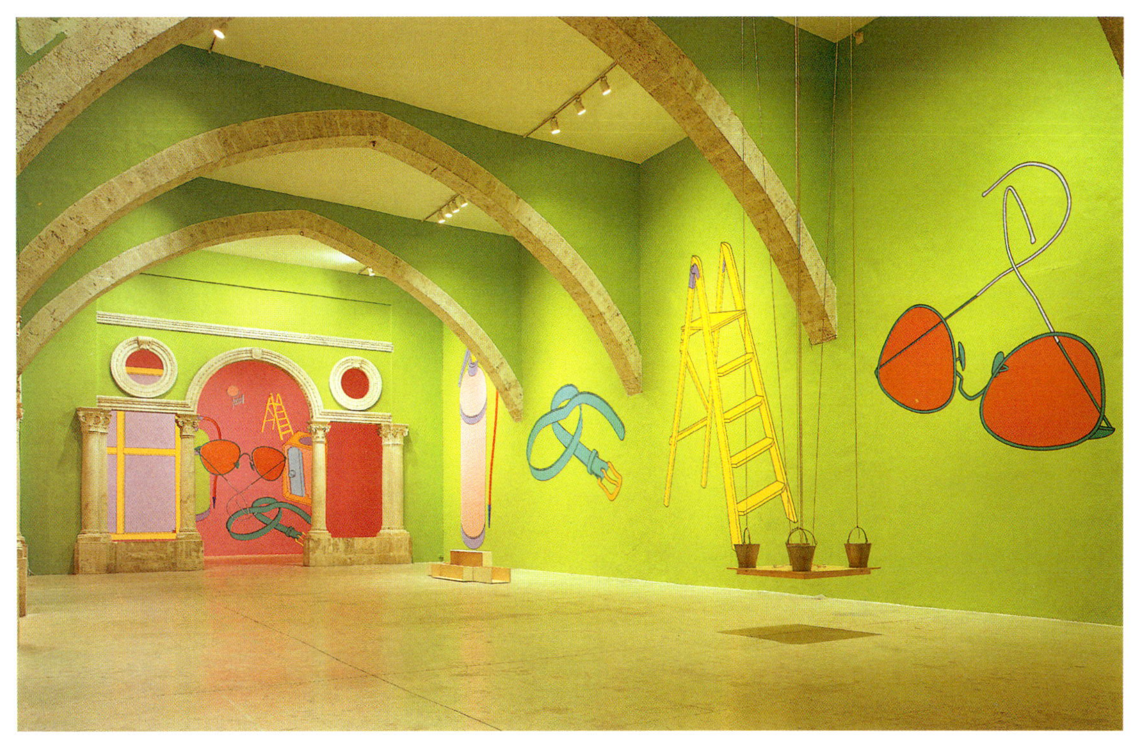

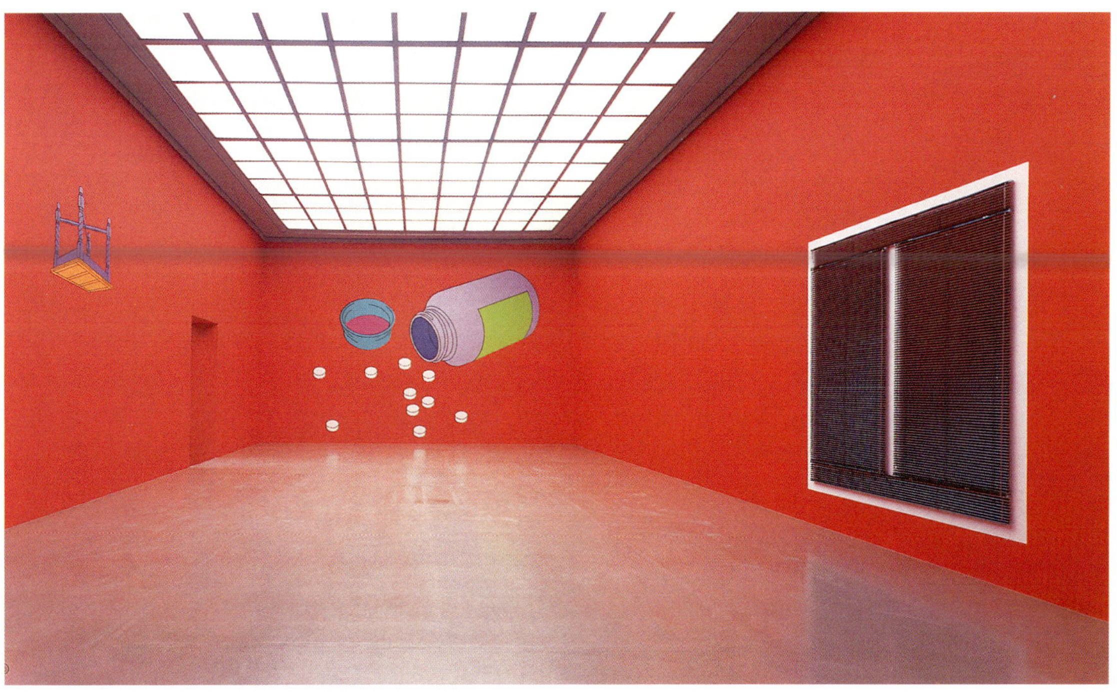

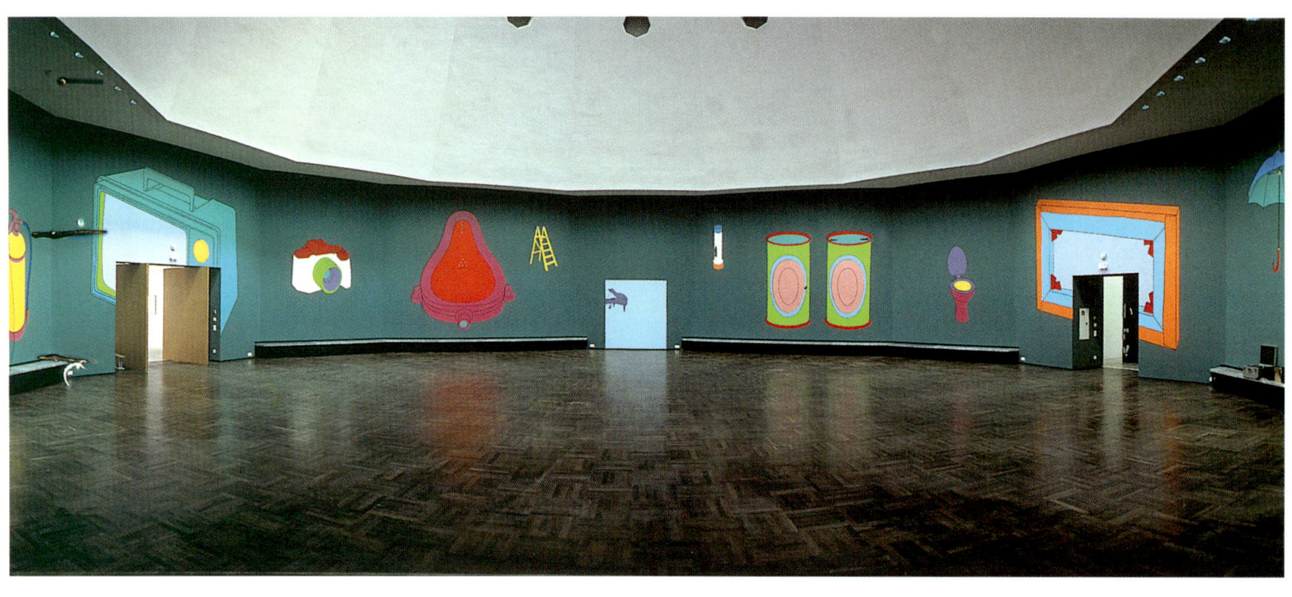

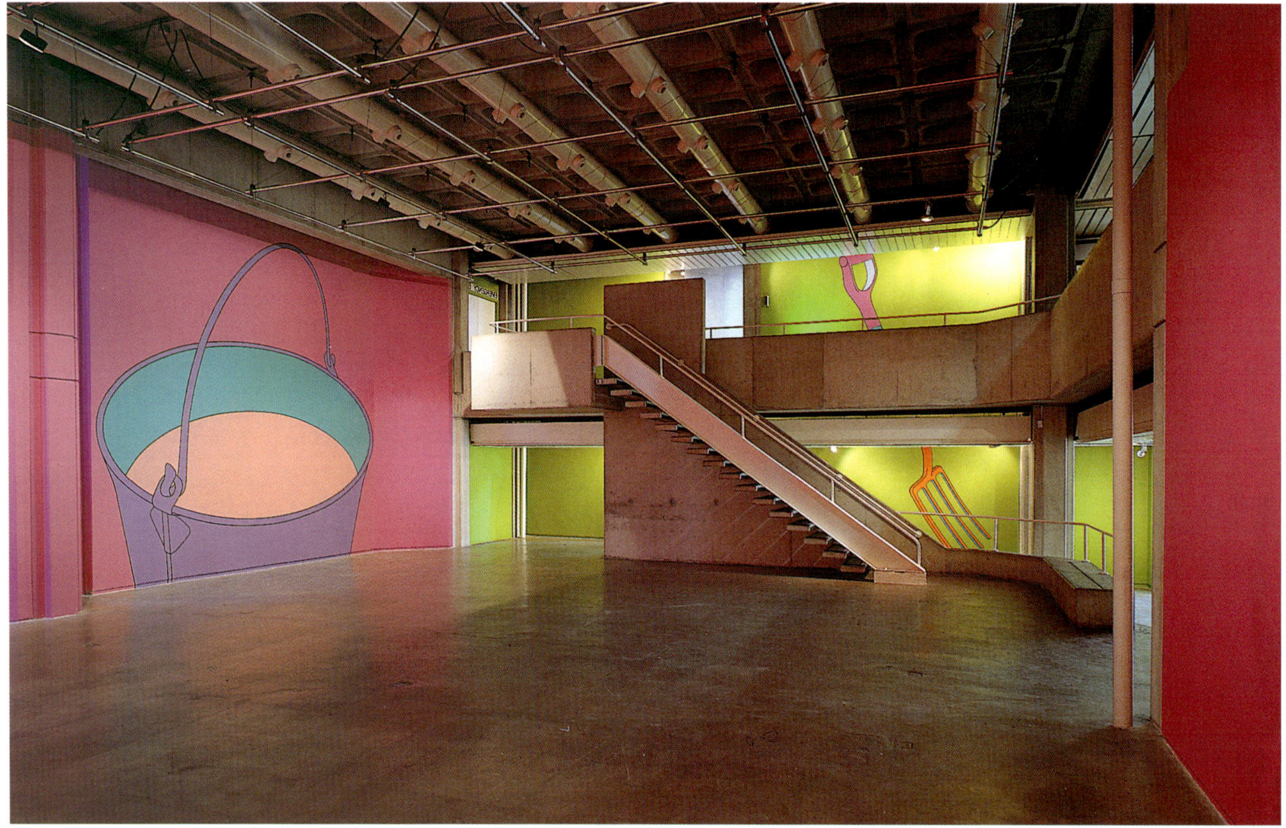

Virginia Button

VB: I'd like to begin by asking how you use the objects in your work. For me they appear to function as words.

MC-M: I see them acting very much as words too. It seems important to say right away that I think of there being a difference between the subject matter and the content of my work.   The subject is the book, the table, the globe...the things. But these are not really what the work is about. Unlike many artists who use real objects in their work I'm not interested in design, I'm not interested in the style of objects, I'm not interested in taste. I see them in a much more abstracted way as language. The objects are very rich in associations, but my use of them is in their assemblage and contextualization. The actual content of my work is about taking these familiar things, and showing to myself as much as to anybody else, that they can offer an unexpectedly wide expressive range. I'm trying to exploit this expressive range as much as possible.

VB: The way you draw an object is very particular, giving the viewer just enough information to recognise and identify its characteristics.

MC-M: Someone just the other day was talking about my 'signature style' of drawing...this was funny, because I deliberately tried to find a way of drawing that didn't have a style. I wanted my images to be as style-neutral as possible. That's why they look mechanistic, why they are always drawn the same, why the line has no inflection, why the line is drawn with tape. They give you just enough information to make it absolutely clear what the object is. Of course it's ironic that if you do anything long enough you get told it's a signature style, and I guess it is!

VB: How you would like the viewer to engage with your objects?

MC-M: My choice of object is always based on the idea that everybody should be able to recognise it immediately. It also needs to have an obvious name - you already have the word on the tip of your tongue - so that any speculation about what it is just doesn't occur. I want you to have an instant sense of familiarity with the thing, and then to pass that first stage of recognition to some kind of second step of actually looking, to consider how things exist in conjunction with another.

I nearly always draw an object more or less the same way from three-quarter perspective, seen slightly from above. It's the most generalised, three-dimensionally readable image. This means, for instance, that the viewer can begin to place the objects on a plane, and they start to infer that there actually is a surface they are sitting on, even though there is no surface. And one begins to ask questions. Is something small but on the same plane as the thing that looks bigger, or is it a big thing far away? Questions that some might consider banal about how we read images seem profoundly interesting to me.

I've always wanted to make what occurs when we look at something unavoidably obvious, so that you can dissect what's happening. I try to make things transparent, exposed. I'd like it to be as if everything was slowed down, so you could watch yourself putting together what it is to understand something, actually watch yourself trying to figure out: 'So that's the perspective. So where is this in relation? So what is this object? What is it for, in relation to that object? This is exactly how we operate, how we make sense of the world. But we don't often have the chance to see ourselves in operation.

VB: Does this involve trying to suggest a presence for the object?

MC-M: My work is largely predicated on the question of presence and about the experience of the present moment. Usually representations of things refer in some way to a situation and a time other than the one the viewer is in at the moment of viewing. You are looking at a landscape that you are not in. You are cast back into some world, or taken to a world where you are not. What I'd like my work to say is 'You are in it, this is it, you are already in that landscape, there's no place else being referred to'.

VB: In relation to this I'd like to ask about your attraction to art of an earlier period, the Renaissance. For me, works of that period have a strong sense of presence.

MC-M: I am interested in a lot of pre-twentieth century art, but in general I prefer early Italian Renaissance artists like Giotto and Piero della Francesca. At that time artists needed a certain simplicity and clarity so that their audience would get the point immediately, and key images, signs, gestures, and narratives were commonly used. I see certain equivalents in our own time about what it is to address a lot of people. For some reason it's what I've always wanted my work to do. With much of my work, if nobody is looking, it doesn't really exist, it's only animated by the presence of the viewer.

VB: A lot of the work made by these artists was site-specific, and has a sense of physicality, which I recognise in your work, particularly through your use of colour. You've talked about your signature style of drawing, but I think your colour is also very distinctive.

MC-M: I try to use colour to confront you with an intensely charged emotional experience of the moment. I feel that over recent years I've re-discovered something known by artists down the centuries that using colour as artifice can ironically reinforce the sense that a painted image is real. Once when I was a student, we were talking about a fifteenth century painting and I commented on how it transported me back to that time. My tutor said 'don't be ridiculous, paintings don't transport you back to some other time, what happens is that you bring them into the present, into your time'. This made a huge impact on me - what an interesting thought - there's no way you can be transported back...works of art aren't time machines.

What really interests me is that it's we who bring the work into our time. Works of art are not historical documents. It's not that you can't use them as historical documents, but for me that's not the function of art. You can walk into a gallery full of amazing masterpieces by the world's greatest artists, and they can leave you completely indifferent. But just one of them is alive for you, and maybe it's just that day, you've never noticed it before, but right now it enters your world. For me, that is the experience of looking at a work of art.

Primarily, I want my work to produce a sense of wonder and pleasure. I want somebody to walk into the room and be knocked out by it, to be amazed by what they see. This is when I am at my happiest with the work. The colour has a palpable, emotional impact. Frankly, I'm doing everything I can to seduce a person! Having done so, I don't want to disappoint them, but what I'm trying to do is provide leads, or rather possibilities. There is no sustained narrative, but I'm trying to imply the possibility of narrative. There's no sustained symbolism, but sometimes images seem all too obviously symbolic. These are leads that take you so far, but don't ever fully account for things. It's really up to you to make of things what you will.

If I scatter a room with painted images on the wall, I would like it to be as if walking into a room with actual objects lying around. When you are buying a flat perhaps the people have moved out, but they've left a bookcase, there's a magazine or a shoe in the corner, and your immediate impulse is to try to figure out something about the people who lived there. Fundamentally, the most interesting thing about the way people are in the world, for me, is that we try to make sense of everything. We can't stand the idea of not knowing. We have this need to have it all make sense.

VB: So does your work celebrate the insecurity of the familiar world that we know?

MC-M: Modern life has made us conscious of the insecurity and instability of the familiar. We are having to learn to live in a world without the reassurance of a framework of unchanging absolutes. We know we need to be able to adapt constantly.

I'd like to talk about something related to this. One of the things about site-specific work is that each place provides me with certain given propositions. I'm not starting from scratch. If I go to a canvas, to make a painting, it's pretty much up to me to figure out what to do. But if I go to a gallery or other building to make an installation I'm confronted with a certain architectural style, scale, and the particular function of the building. I always see these givens as guides, as triggers for new ideas rather than as impositions or limitations. I don't have to invent them, and they often force me to find a solution I wouldn't have thought of otherwise. So in fact, the constant givens in my work are those of my own orthodoxy - the objects, the colour range, the style of drawing. What's interesting about site-specific work is that you are presented with a new set of concerns.

VB: The piece you're doing for Manchester is inside a building with a very specific purpose and location. How might these givens have affected your thinking about what to do?

MC-M: The new space in Manchester is one of the largest single rooms for showing art in Britain. To be honest, it's a very daunting room. It was difficult to work out how to deal with it, and I think other artists and curators will also find the space formidable. The new development of the Gallery is clearly an attempt to make Manchester a more important location for showing art both nationally and internationally, and as my installation is the inaugural exhibition, I thought it should be celebratory.

I decided to try to make this vast room look even bigger, as though it wasn't quite big enough. So on the largest wall facing you as you come in I'm going to paint separate images of objects, some of which disappear off the ceiling as they appear to recede in space. At the centre of the wall is a painting of the back of a canvas, behind which you can just see bits of a globe. All around is a sea of objects being gravitationally sucked in towards the canvas. When you turn around, there will be a painting on canvas on the opposite wall in which all of the same objects reappear. The painting looks a bit like an attic room filled with random things packed in. The relative scale and the colour of the objects are exactly the same as the objects on the other side of the room. This is why the work is called Inhale/Exhale, because it appears as though everything has been sucked in and then blown out.

VB: There seems to be a sense of movement in Inhale/Exhale between the wall and the canvas. Might this suggest a directional pull in your work between the practices of wall installation and painting on canvas?

MC-M: Yes. In essence, this is what I have been doing in my work over the past few years. That is, I am going back and forth between wall painting and the canvas. I feel I've come to painting in possibly the oddest possible route, because I've gone through everything else from making constructions, to working with actual objects, to neon, wall drawings, and then painted rooms, which finally gave me a way into making paintings.

VB: Some people might find it curious that you've found it so difficult to move towards painting.

MC-M: At the beginning of my career my resistance to painting was very strong, not because painting was dead, but painting seemed full. It had all been done. So by the end of the 1960s hardly any of the interesting art being made was to do with painting. But more importantly for me, I have needed the path I am on to unfold in a way that makes sense to me. I haven't known where that path is going, but I get a sense that this is acceptable to me, and that isn't. I couldn't have painted images like this twenty years ago as it didn't make sense to me at that time.

VB: Going back to Inhale/Exhale...The reversed canvas painted on the centre of the wall looks just like a window, a window on the world...

MC-M: The image of the reversed canvas is the key to the work. Everything passes through it. And it can indeed be seen to be a window on the world beyond the gallery.

VB: Actually, I think what you are addressing here is something very fundamental about picture-making, particularly as there is a real canvas opposite.

MC-M: Yes. It is an exercise about the nature of painting, about the relationship of painting to the world. The objects I use in my work are drawn from real things - they are my attempt to make images as close as possible to being real and having the presence of the real. So in the installation in Manchester the objects painted on the wall are in a sense the 'real things', which then appear as 'images' on the painted canvas opposite.

VB: You've worked with some of the same objects for about twenty-five years now. Have you noticed them changing in any way?

MC-M: Something has started happening that makes me feel uneasy. I started drawing the objects in the late seventies. Many were objects that I had. It wasn't my intention to make them personal, but they were, for example, the actual keys to my flat. But increasingly the objects look dated, a bit old-fashioned. When I look at contemporary objects now, it's clear that the ones I use came from the period of design when the objects looked like the thing that they did. Form and function were really very close. If we look at my electronic car key, it doesn't look like a key at all, it looks more like a calculator. And a calculator looks like a mobile phone, and the phone looks like a computer and the computer like a microwave, and so on. Increasingly the world we are creating is a world in which objects are not a visualisation of the function they perform. Everything looks more or less alike.

VB: Why is function expressed through form so important to you?

MC-M: I have always been very intrigued by such questions as why is it that we recognise bits of wood assembled in a certain way as a chair, but when there is another bit of wood sitting on top of the chair, we know it's not part of the chair. How do we know this?

VB: Through experience perhaps?

MC-M: Yes, it's partly to do with experience, and to do with language, how we understand the formulation of things. What would happen if we took all the bits that made the chair and laid them out? There wouldn't be a chair. It wouldn't exist. It's only a chair when it takes the form of a chair. Questions like that have always interested me.

VB: So your objects are metaphors for the way we think, the way we understand things by putting bits, or rather words, together?

MC-M: That's why I have always been fascinated by Wittgenstein's exploration of language. He takes a simple phrase or sentence and shows that by changing the position of a single word its inflection and meaning is changed completely. This is the model for what I try to do. The images painted on the wall are one thing, the same images crowded into the canvas mean something entirely different.

VB: Wittgenstein advocated the idea of the 'word-game' in order to unmask what might underpin our understanding of words. He developed strategies for penetrating the familiar use of language, so that he could become more self-aware of its limitations as a system for understanding things. Do you see yourself using word-games in this sense?

MC-M: Very much so. This relates to my earlier work the Oak Tree. In written language, the word table doesn't look anything like a table. By the same token, I can draw a table but use it like a person. It can become a figure. The fact that it doesn't look like a person is not the relevant question. It doesn't have to look indistinct or amorphous for you to read it as a figure. It can look inescapably like a table, and yet I can put it into a context that looks like an assembly of people. And within that it becomes one of the people. Language allows us extraordinary flexibility in how something is understood.

In visual language this is to do with our ability to see something as a picture. For example, I can draw a table, we have no table, but we have the experience of the presence of the table without the table being present. The question of it being perceived by us as a table is not a quality of the drawing, but a capacity in us. We can look at the clouds and see a face, we can look at a shadow and see a person, we can look at a drawing of a table and see a table, because a strange capacity in us allows us to see one thing as another. This makes us much more active in our relationship to understanding images than we assume, less passive. This realization has been crucial for me. Making this activity self-conscious is what I've been trying to get at. It's why I try to give clues...it's to allow the exercise of one's full capacity to read the thing. I present you with something that seems obvious, so that you can hopefully get a sense of what it is you are actually doing when you construct something out of it.

VB: In a sense that's why your work is so demanding...it doesn't allow you to switch off. It can be quite uncomfortable.

MC-M: I try to use all the pleasures of colour and scale and humour I can to engage the viewer in an experience of the present where everything happens at once and at full intensity. But because this saturated moment is frozen, put on hold so that you can move around in it, the ultimate experience can indeed be unsettling or unnerving in an unexpected way. Beauty always has another side, doesn't it?

9.00am 2.4.2002

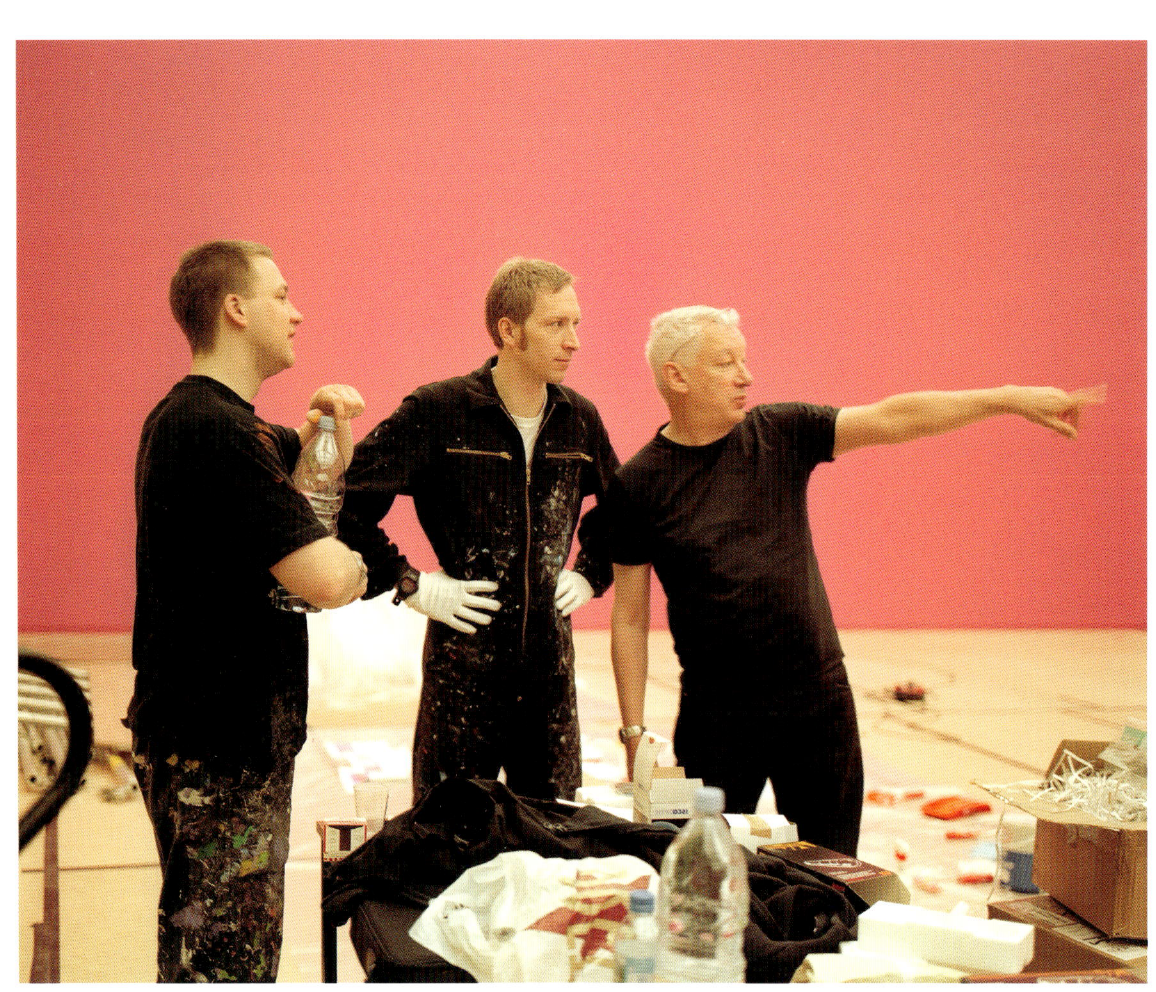

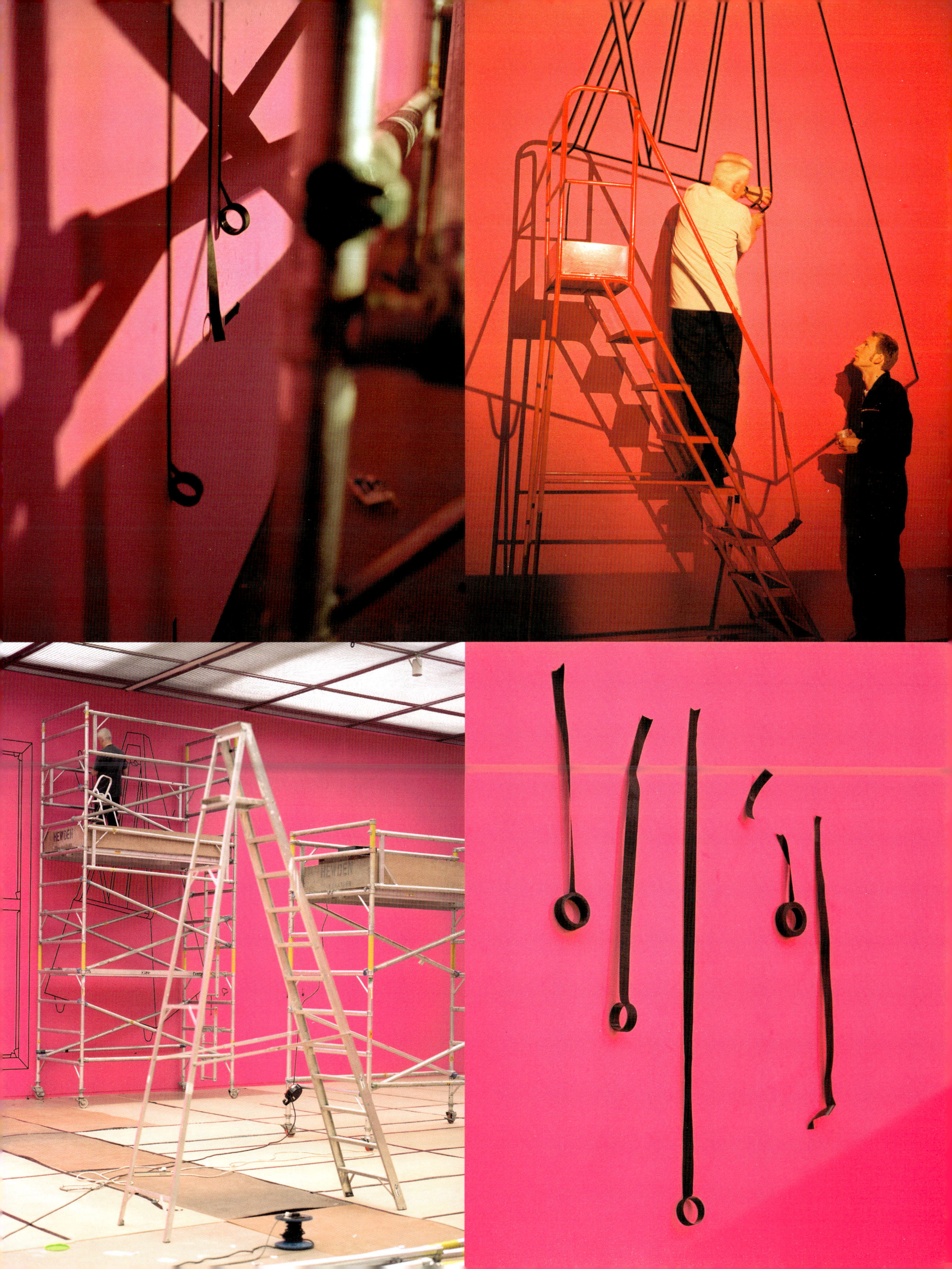

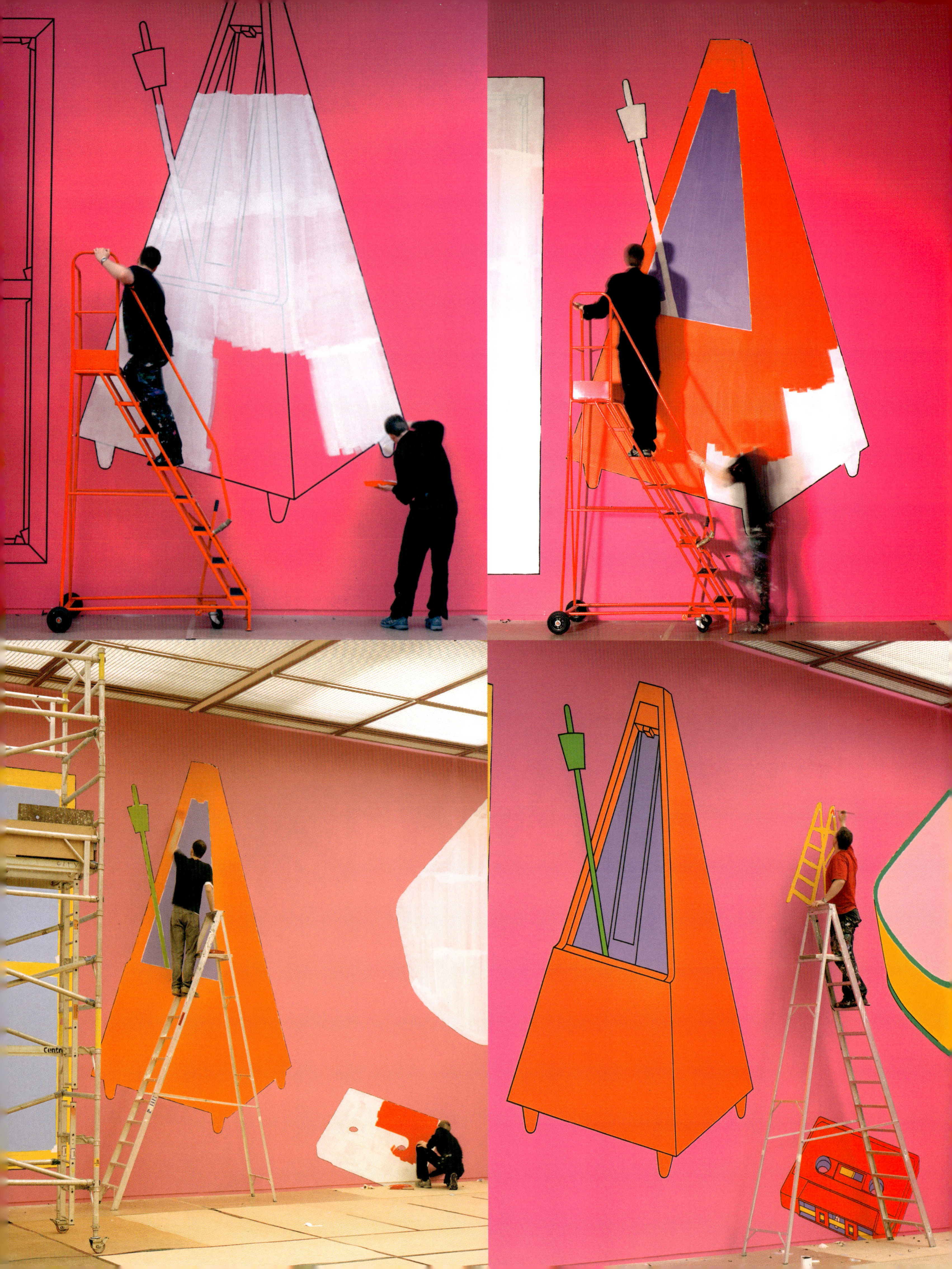

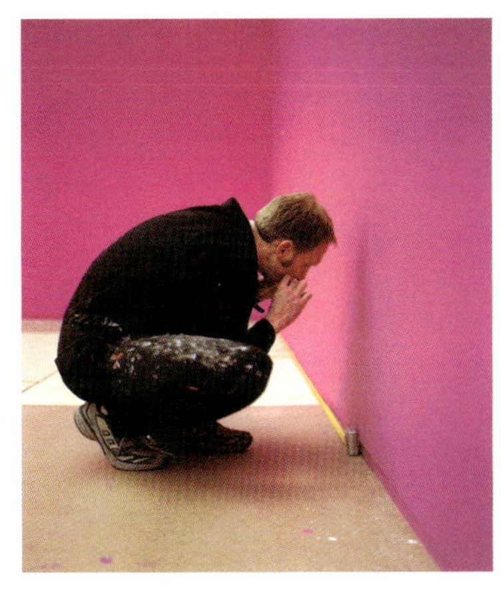
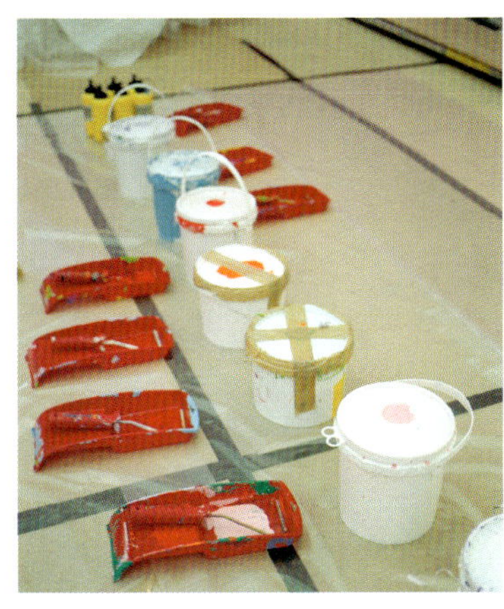
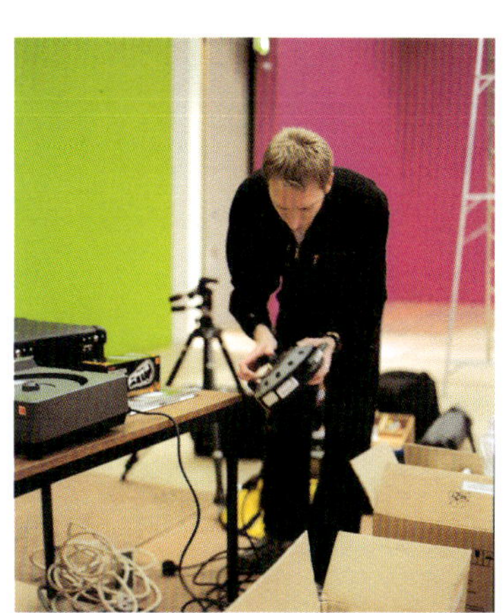
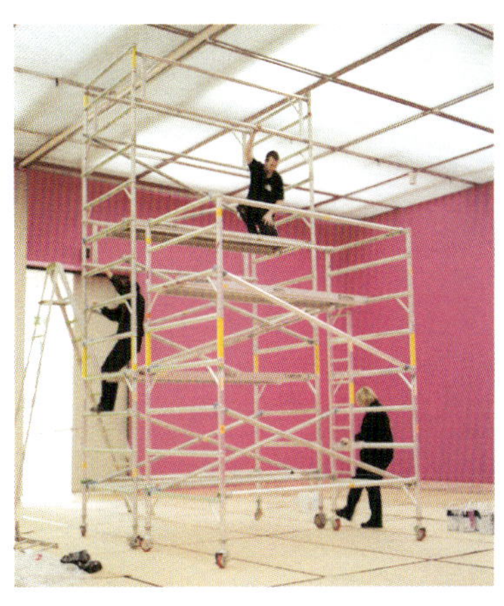
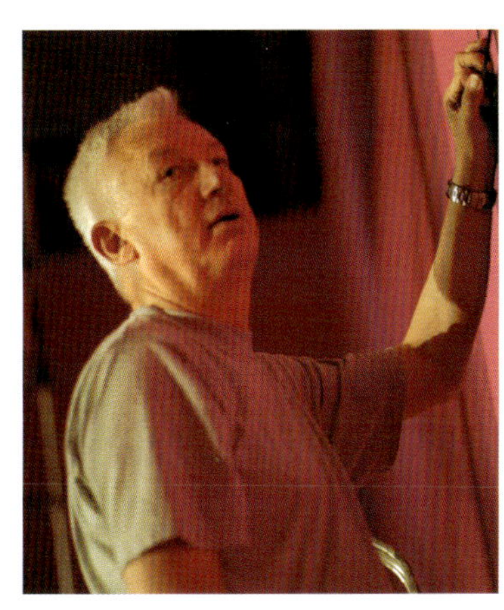
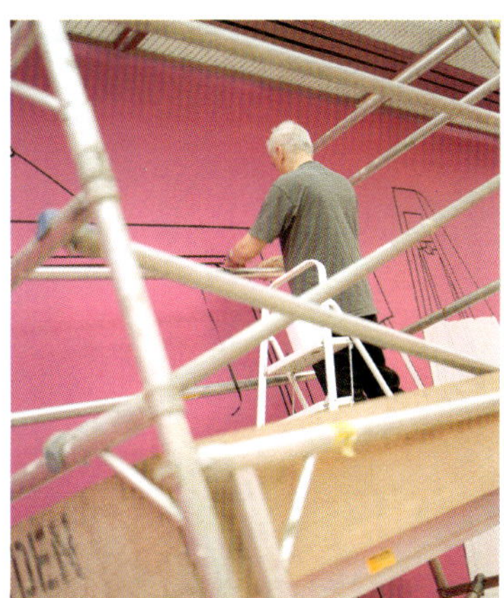
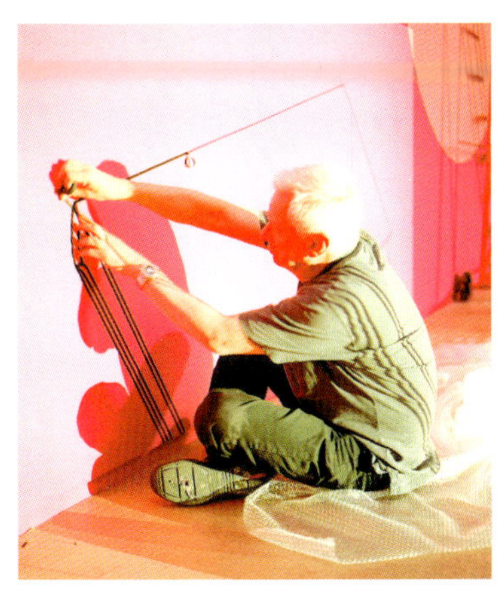
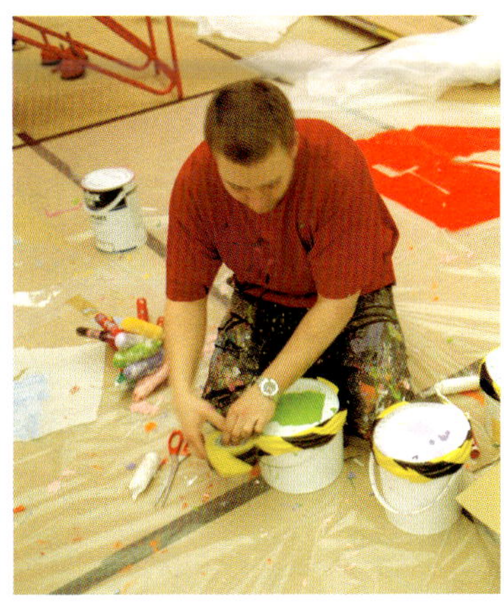
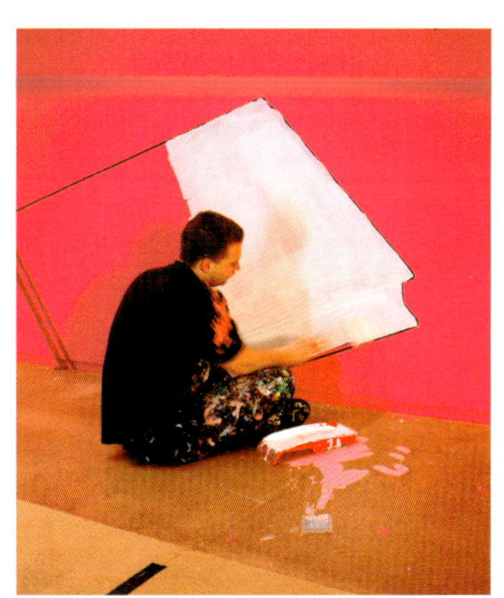

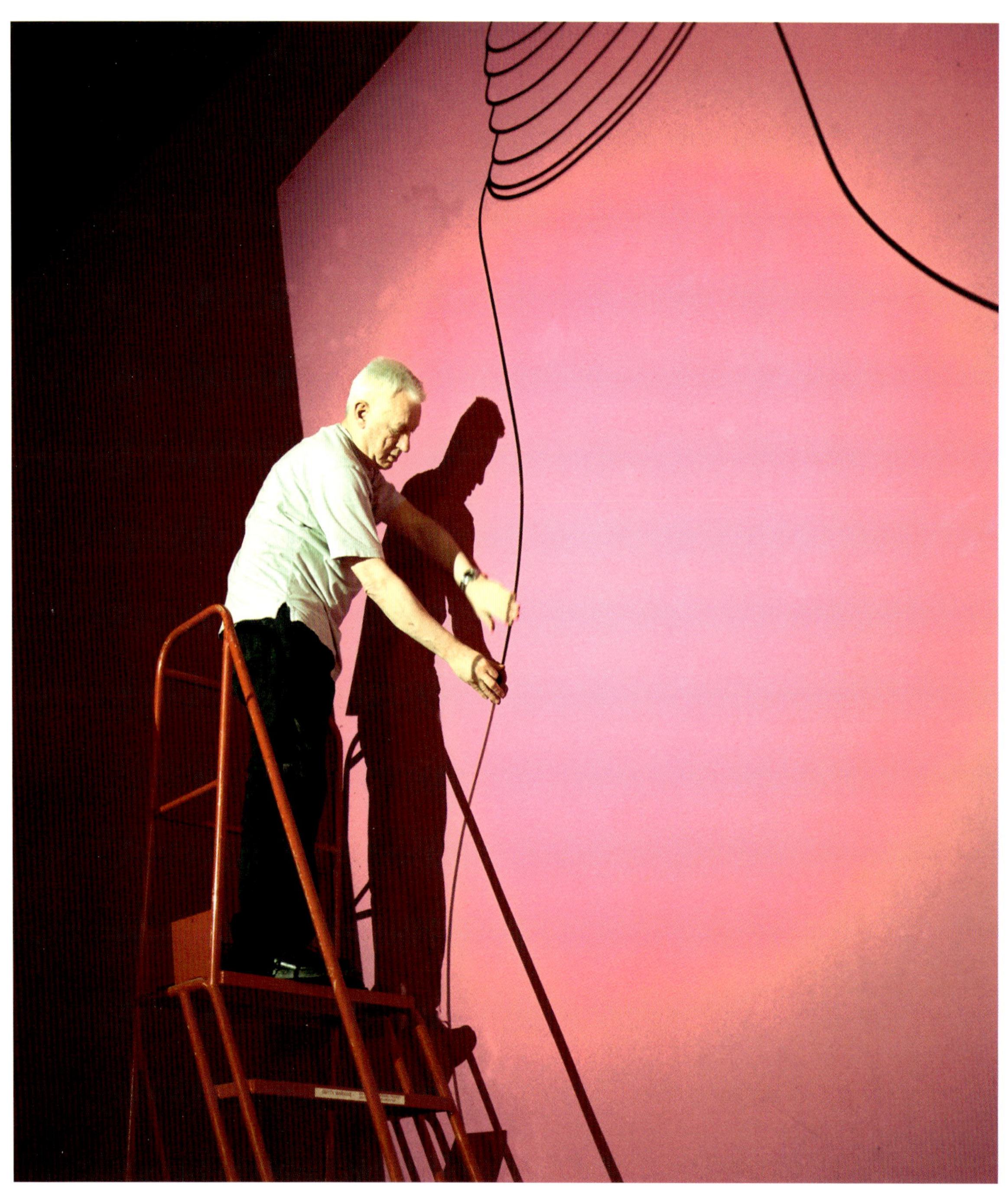

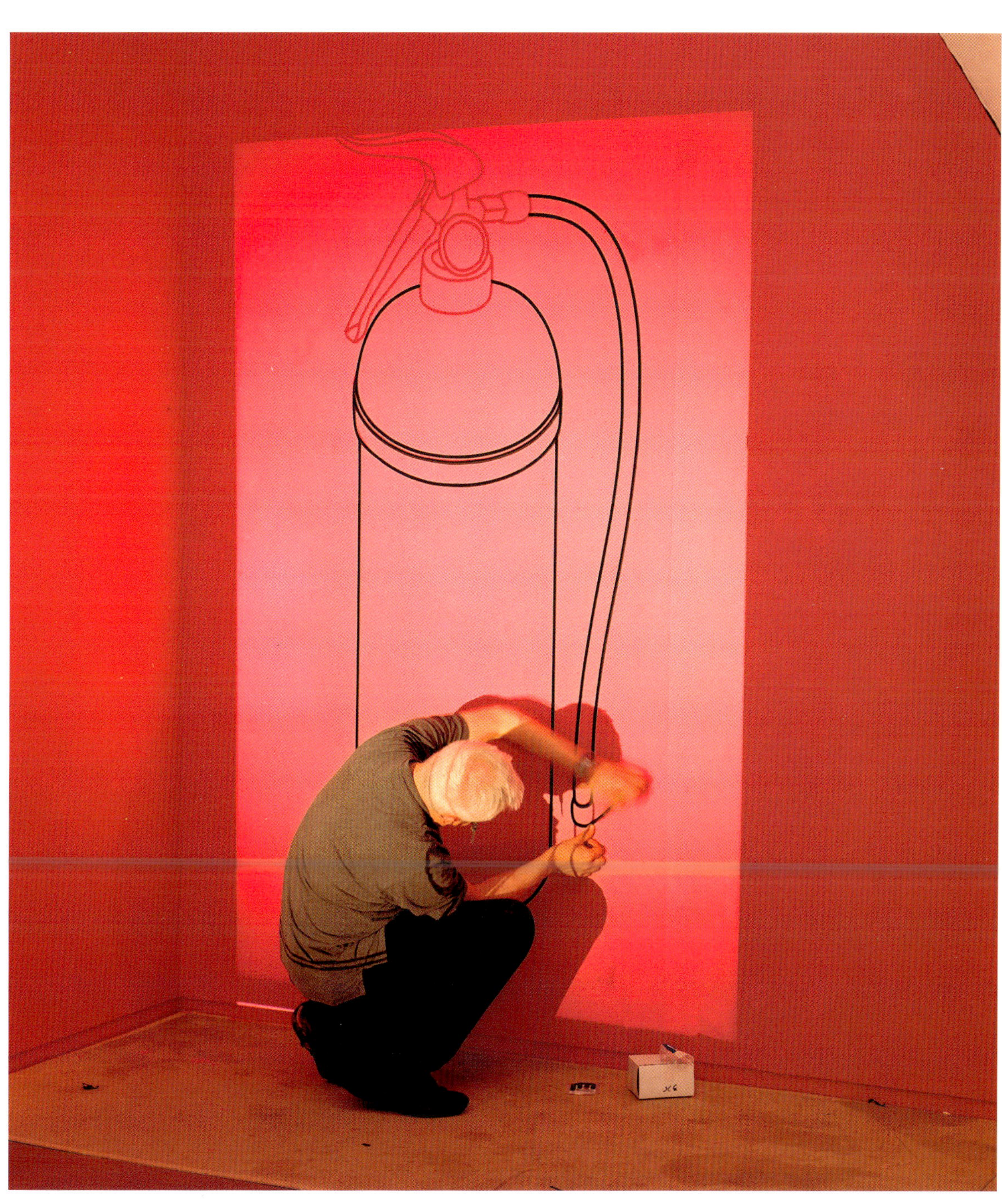

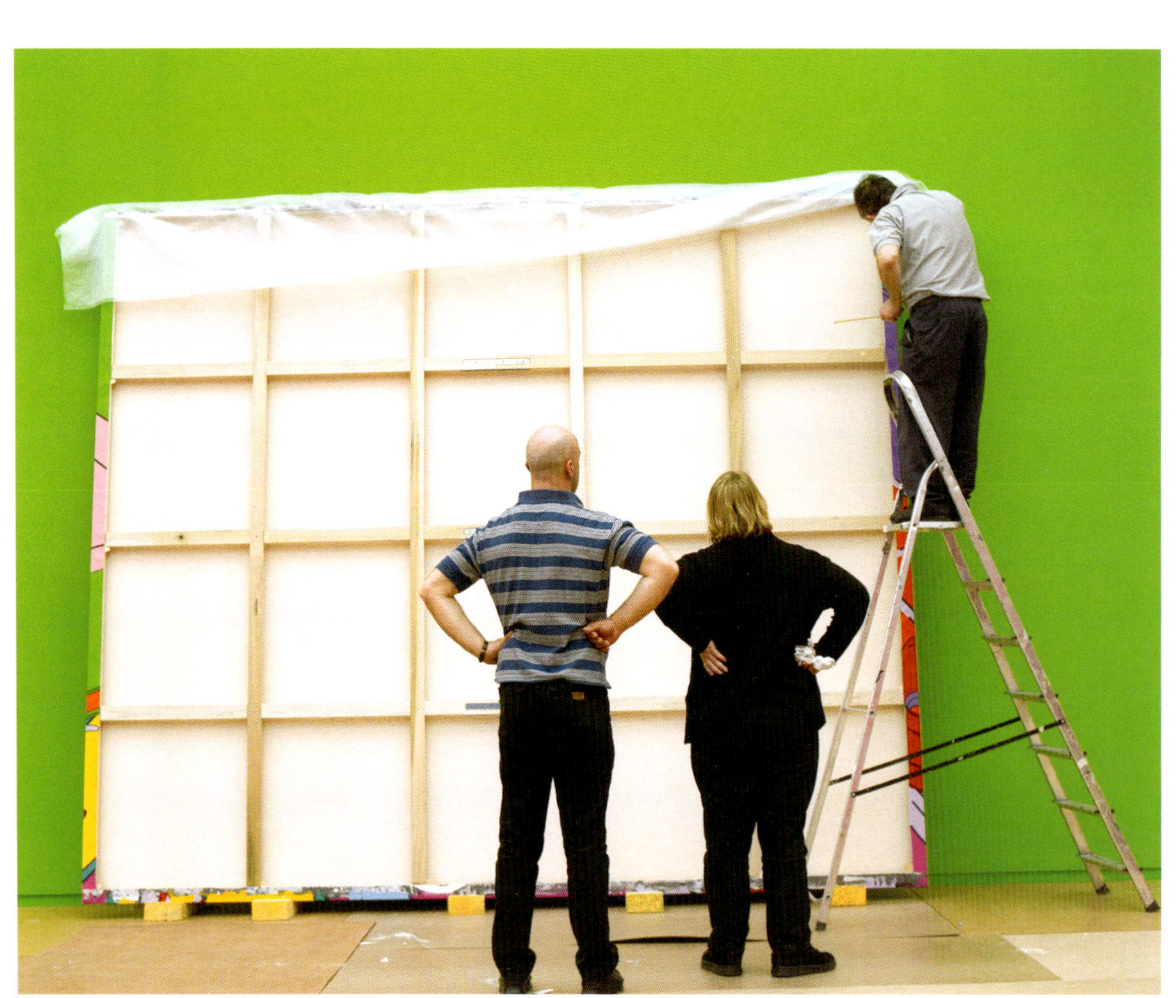

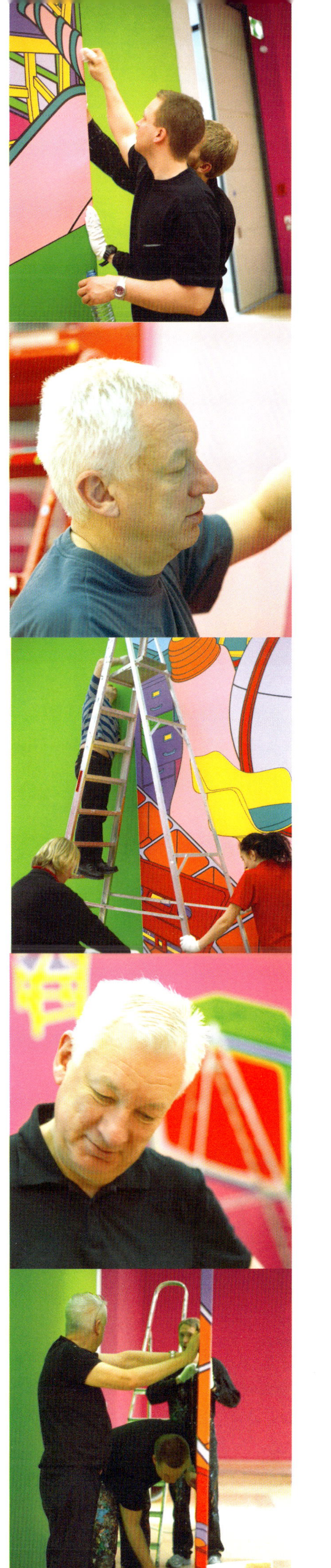

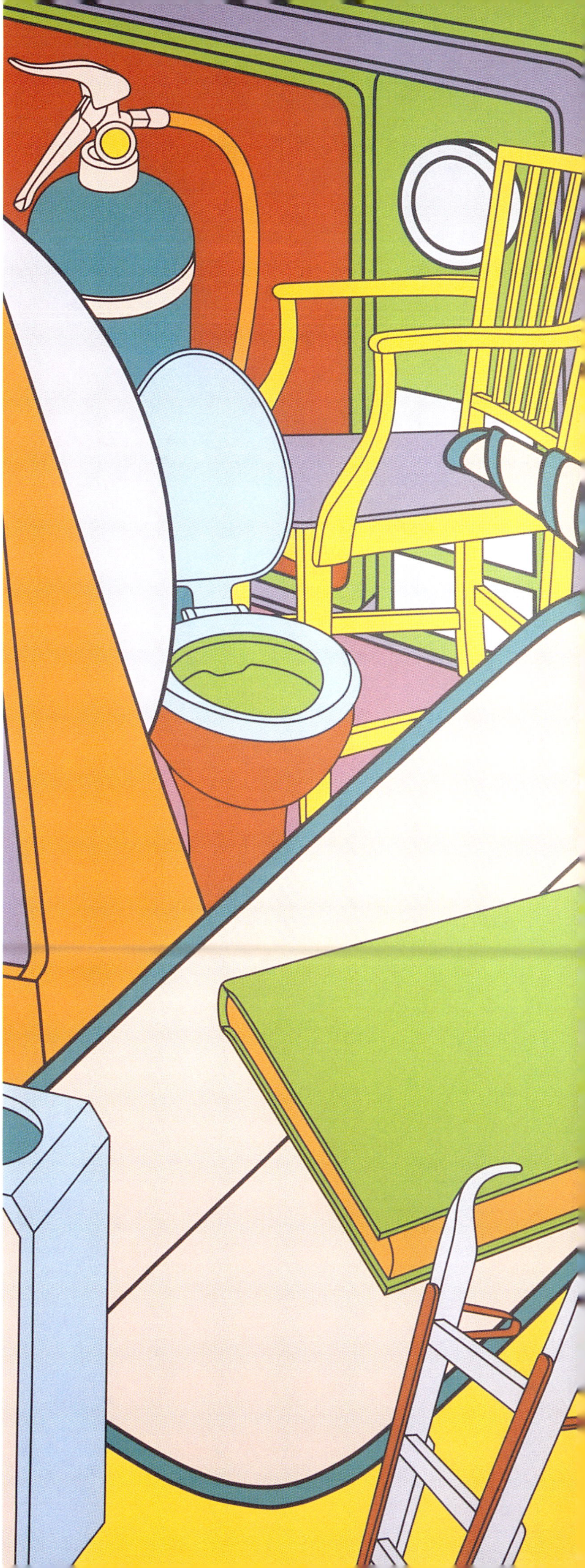

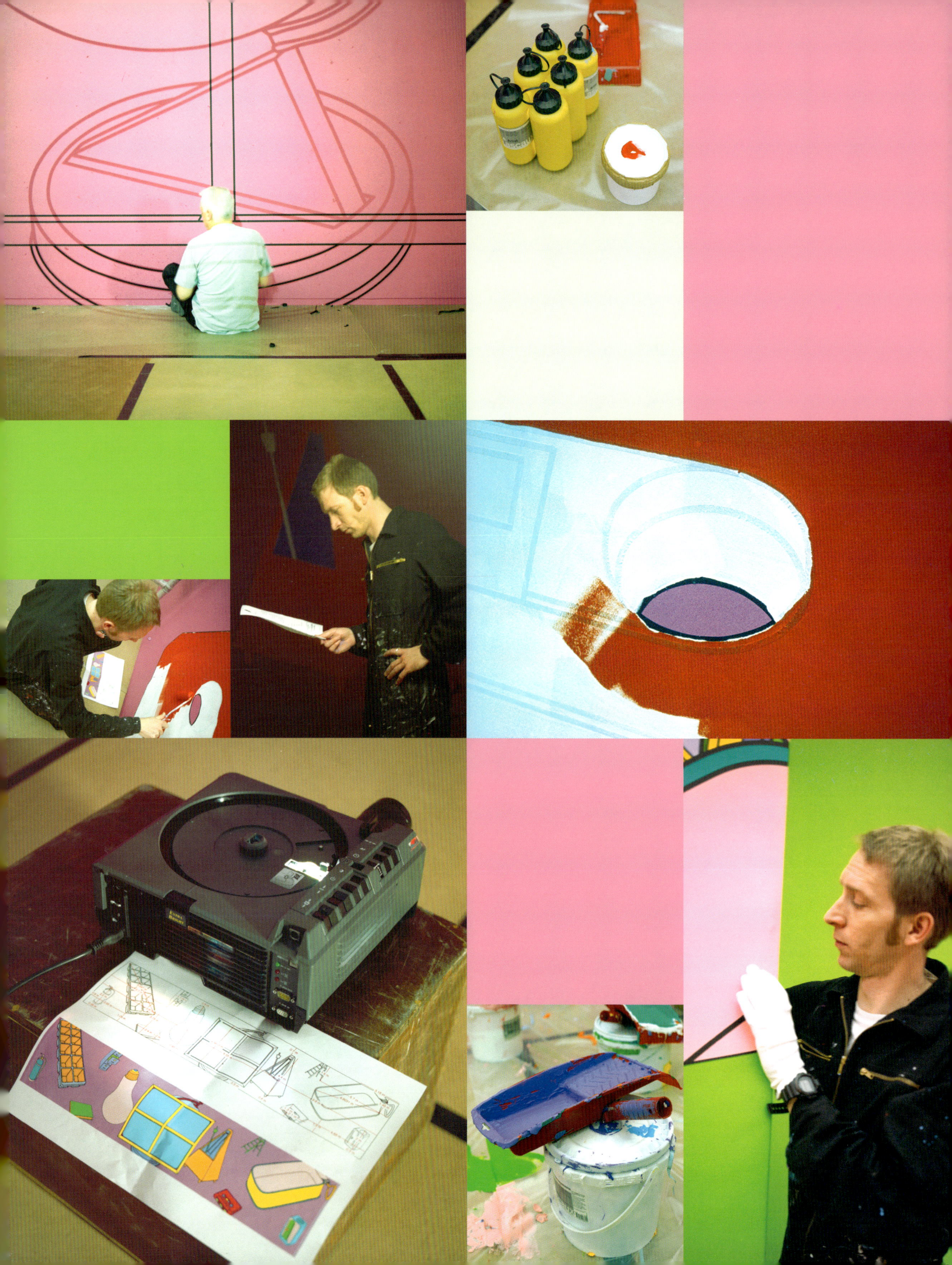

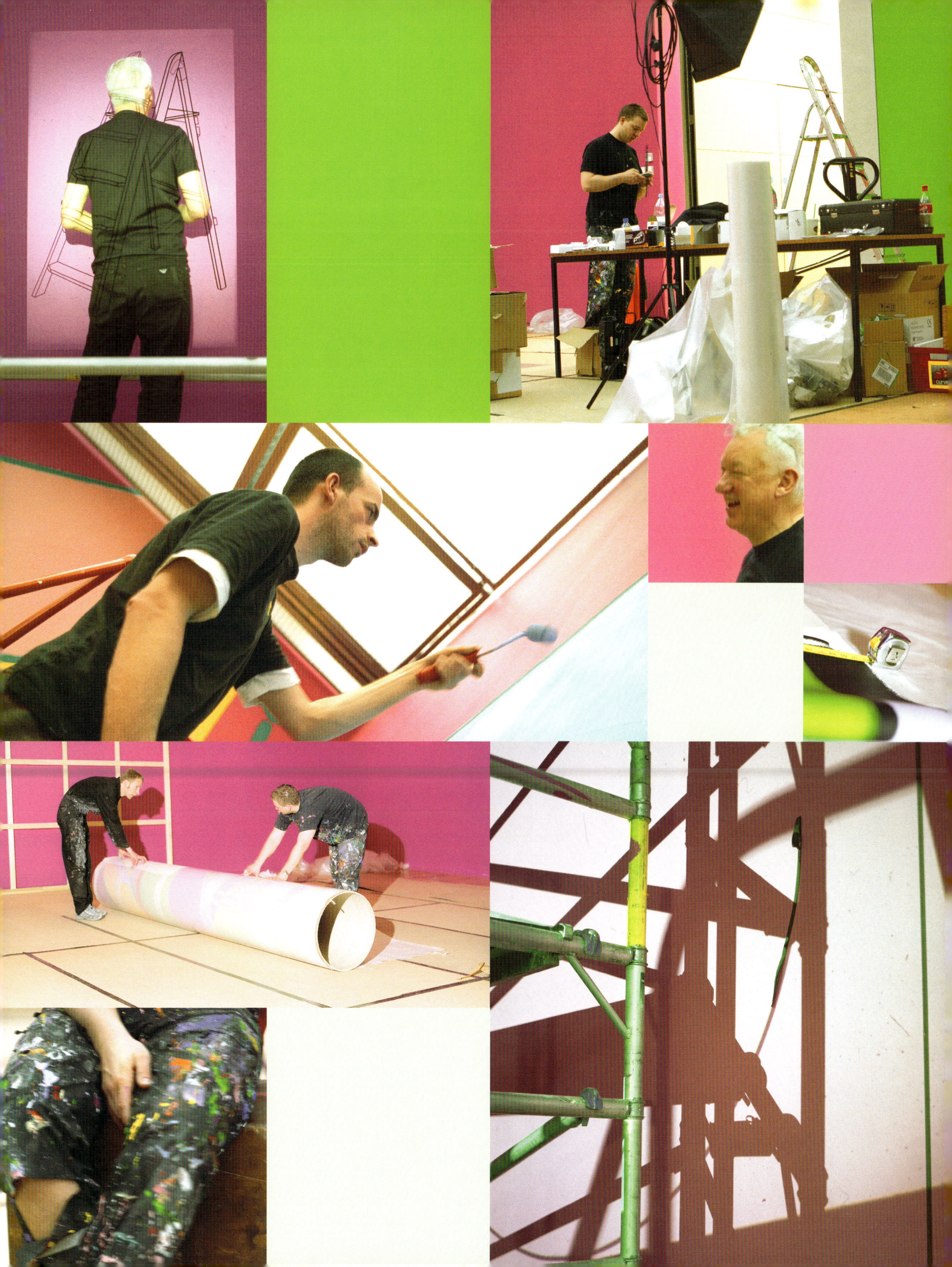

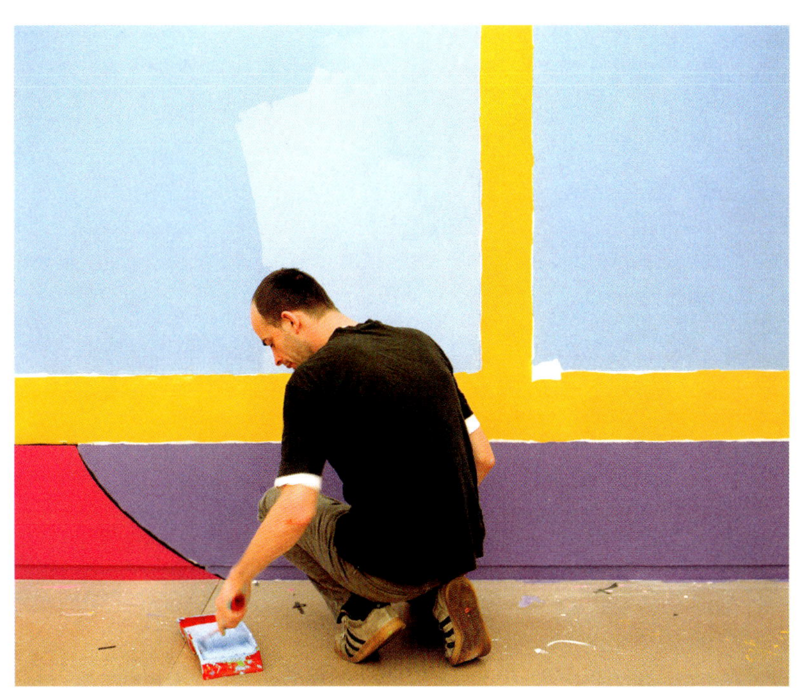

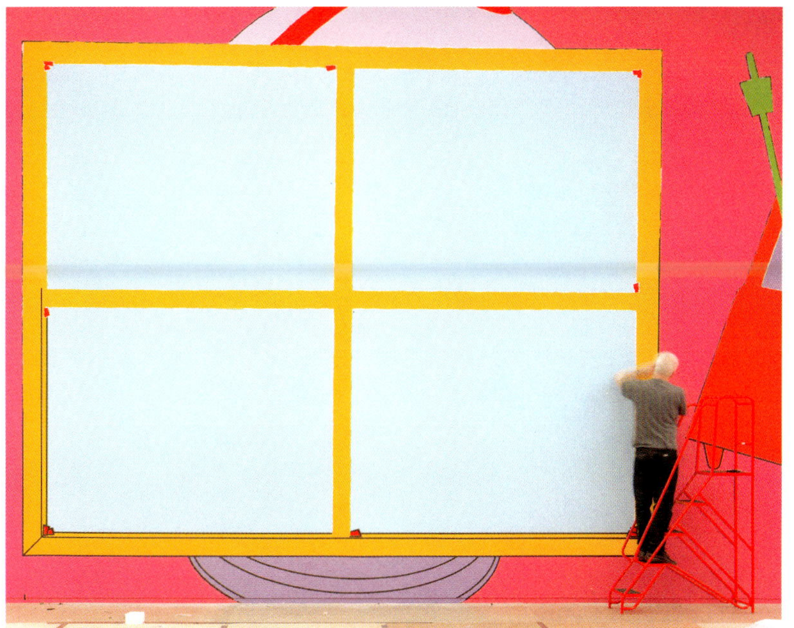

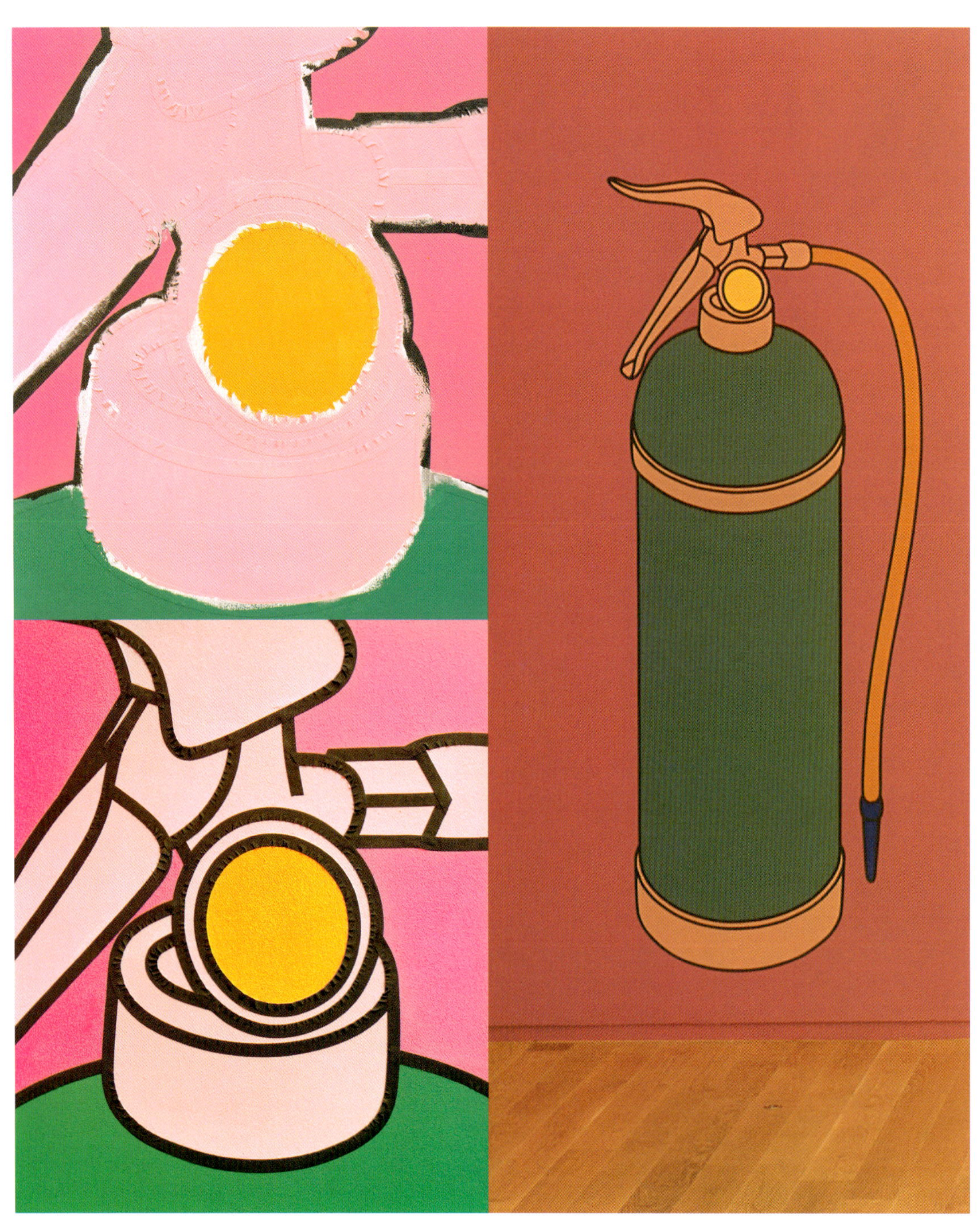

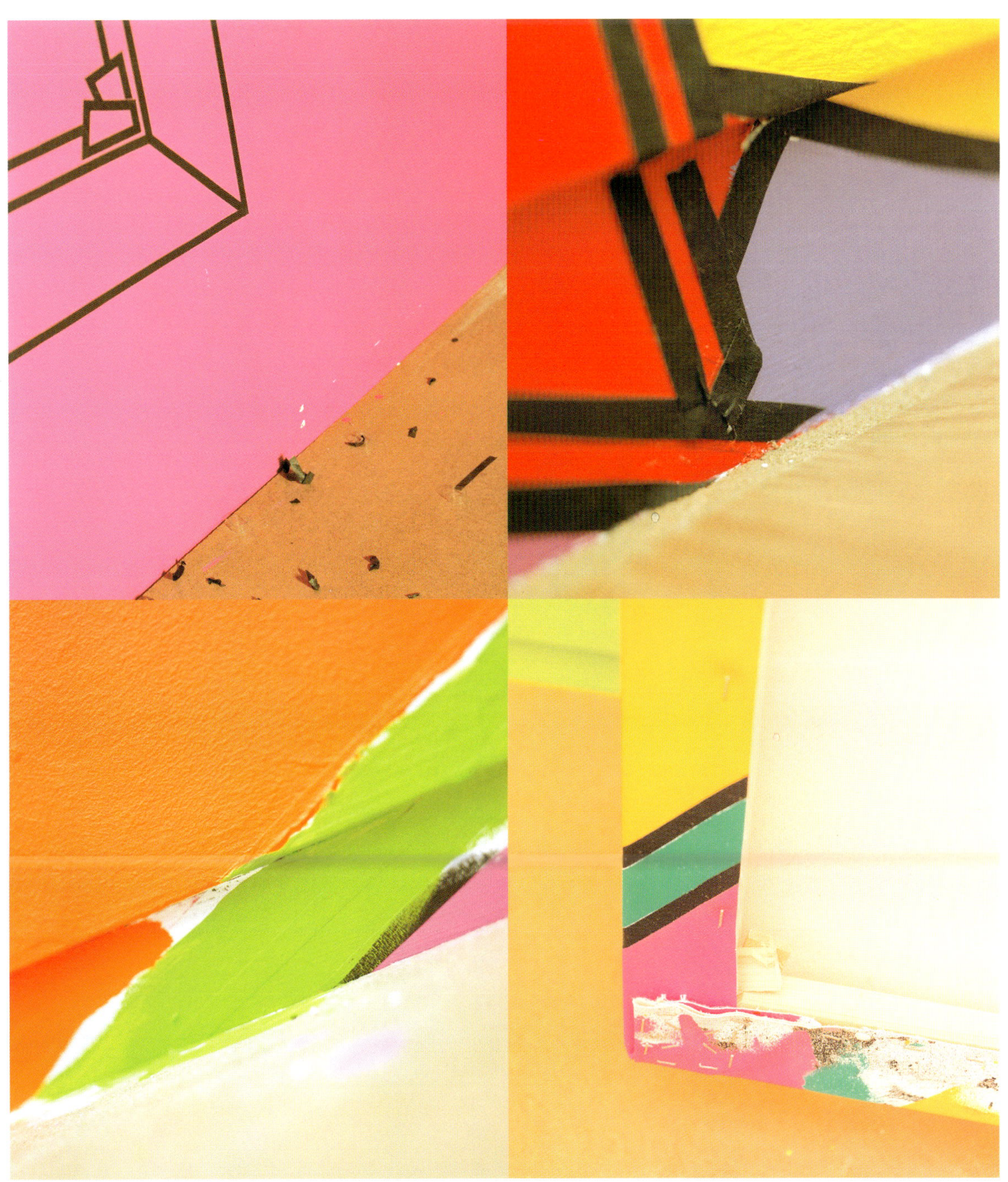

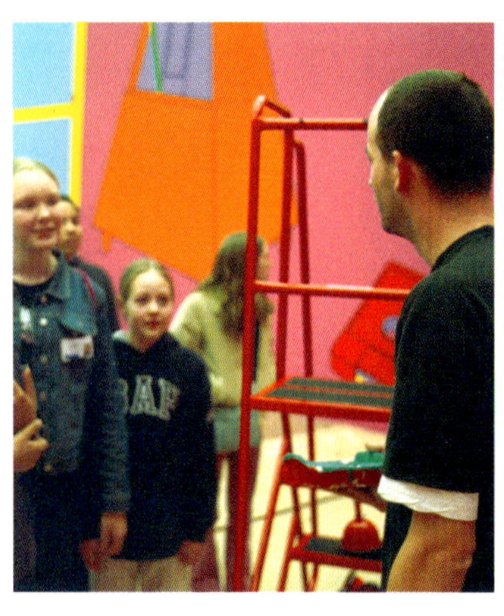
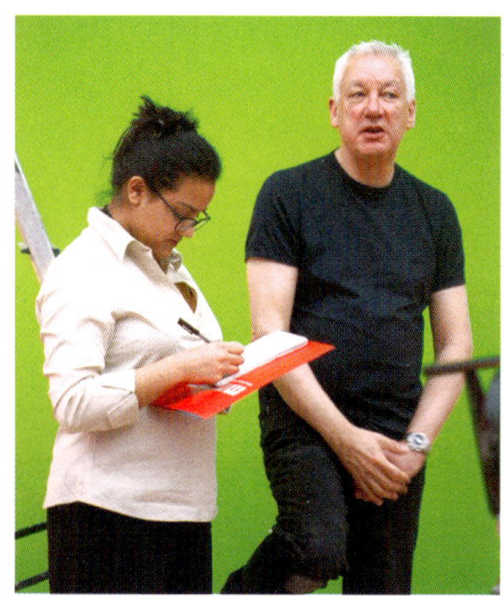
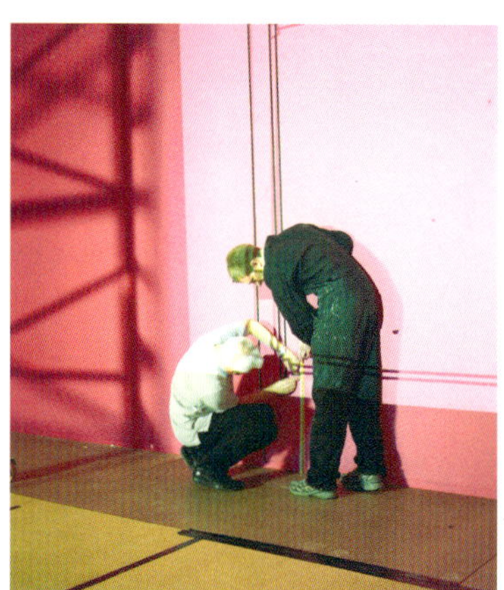
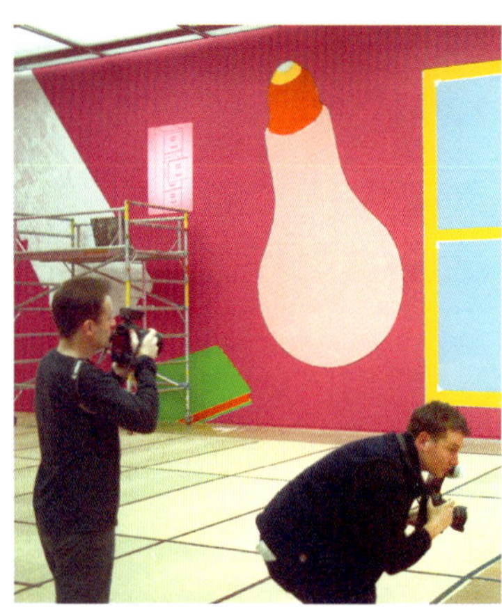
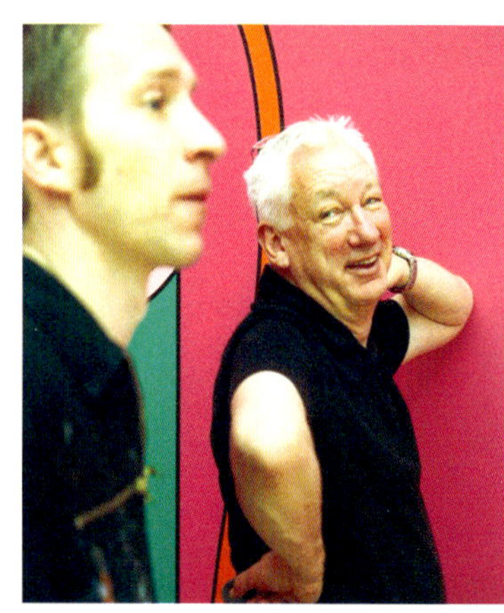
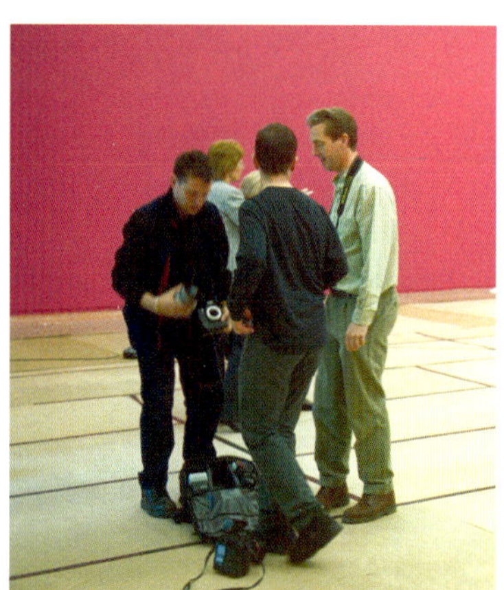
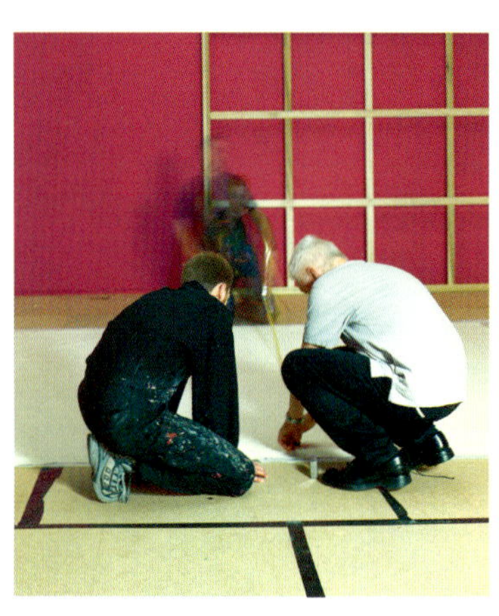
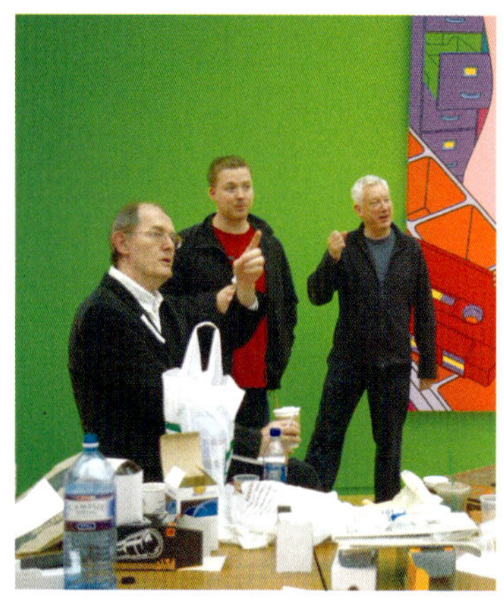
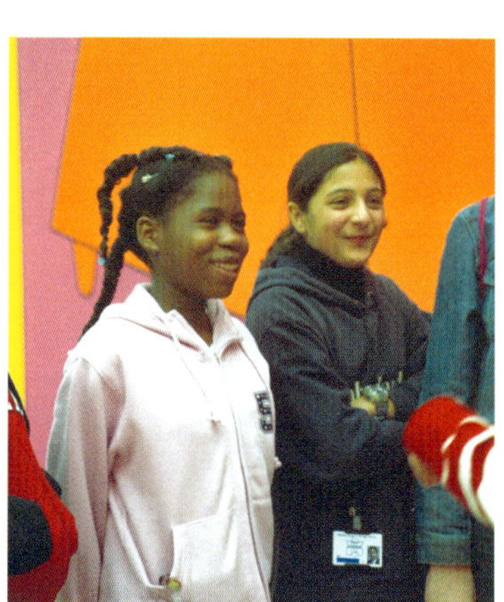

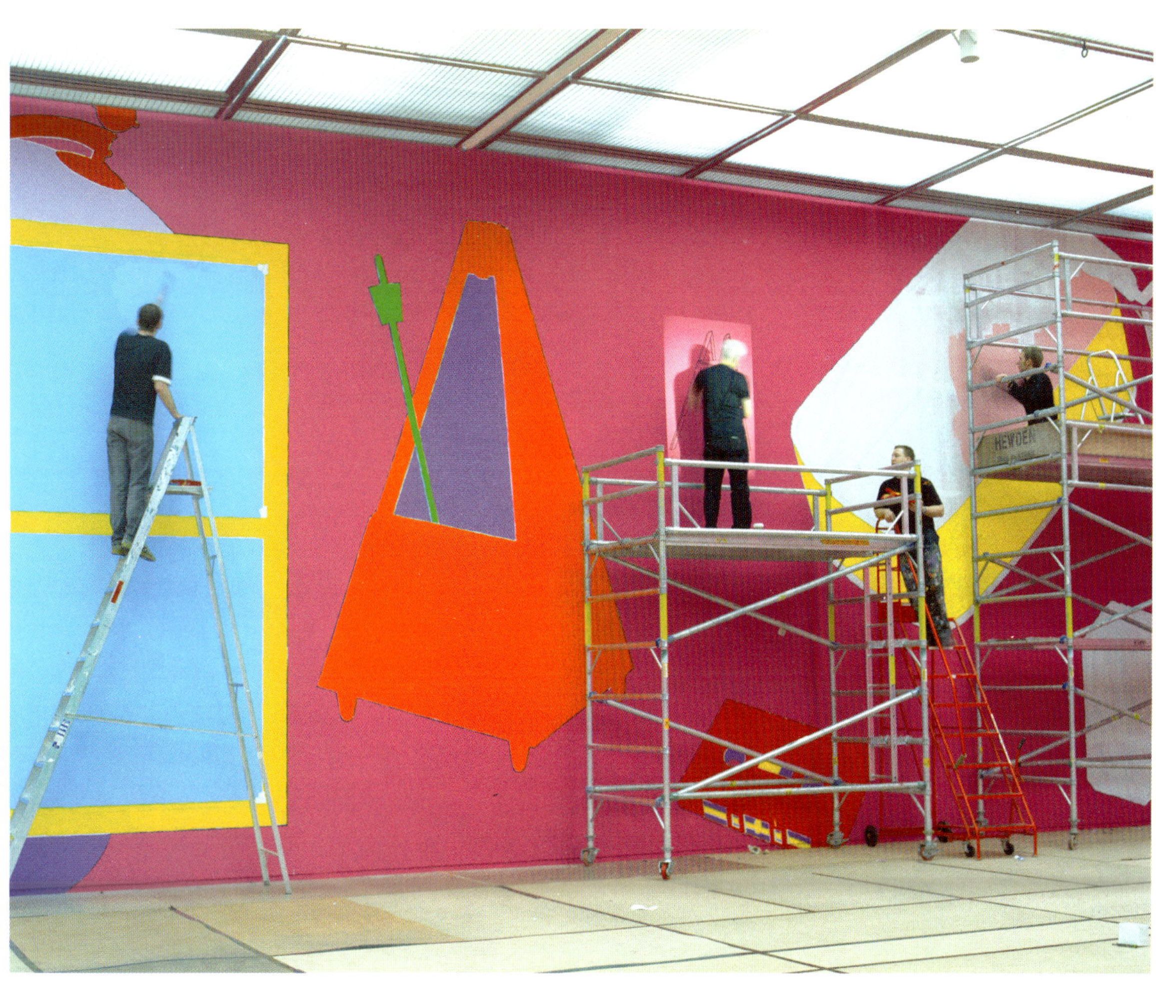

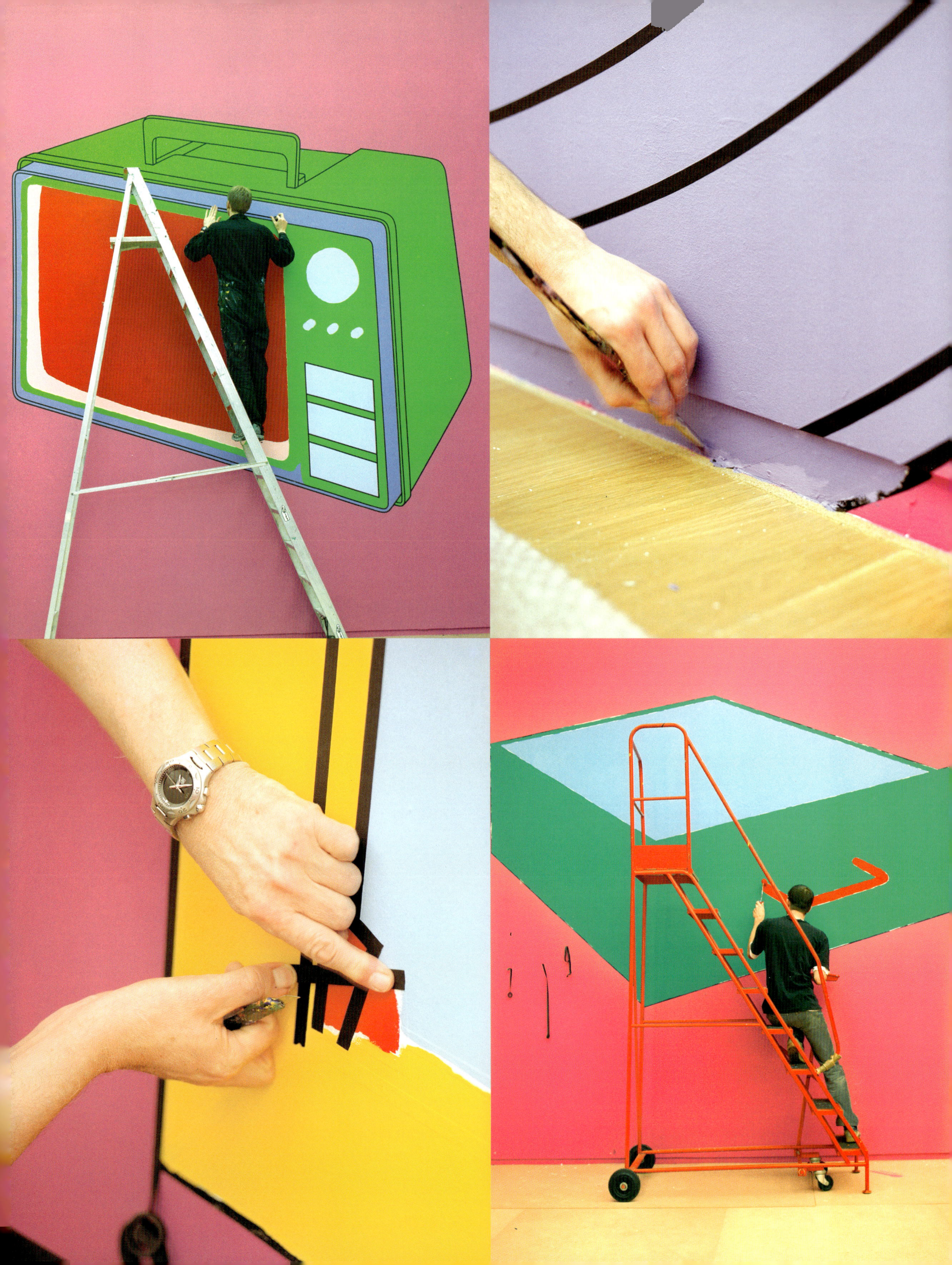

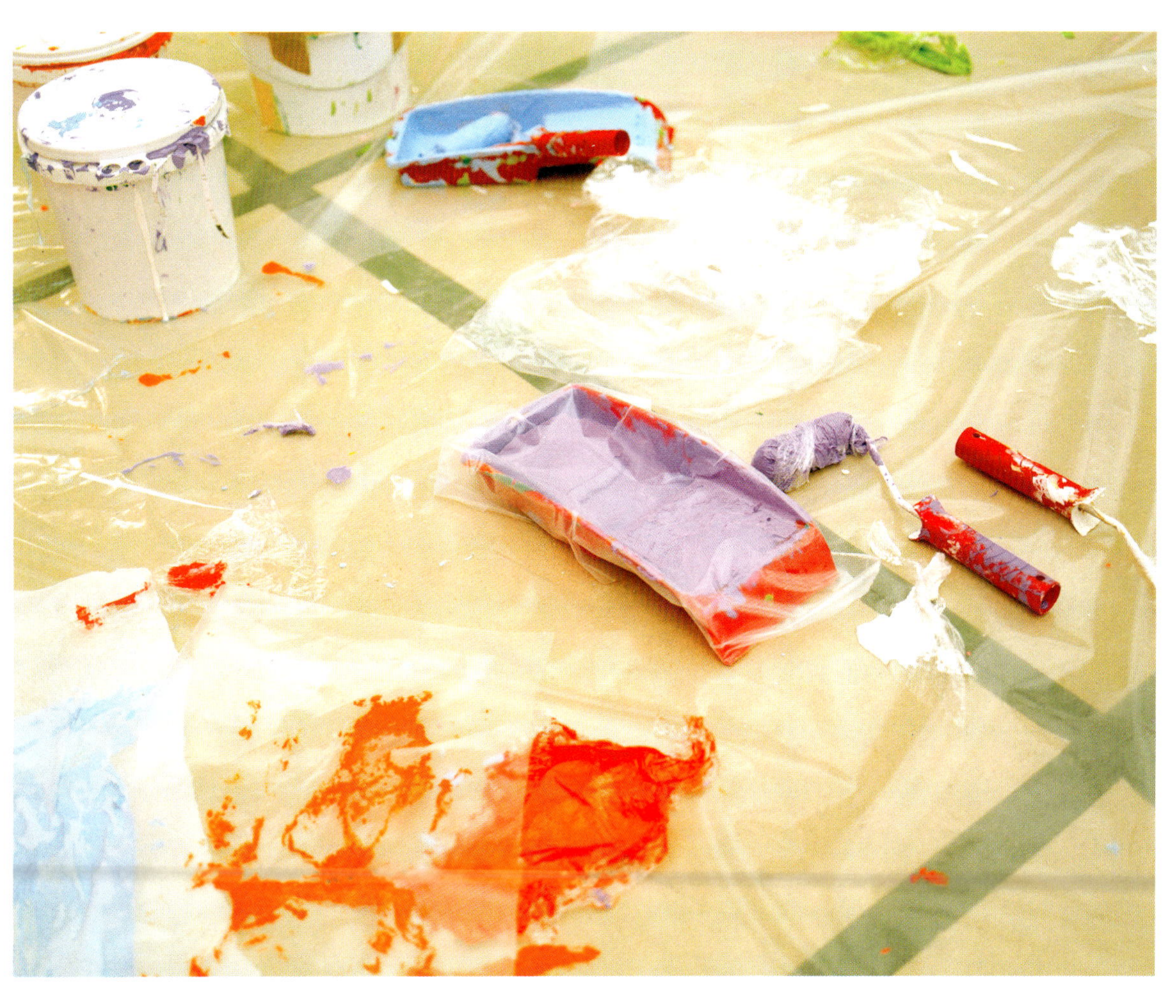

4.30pm 6.4.2002

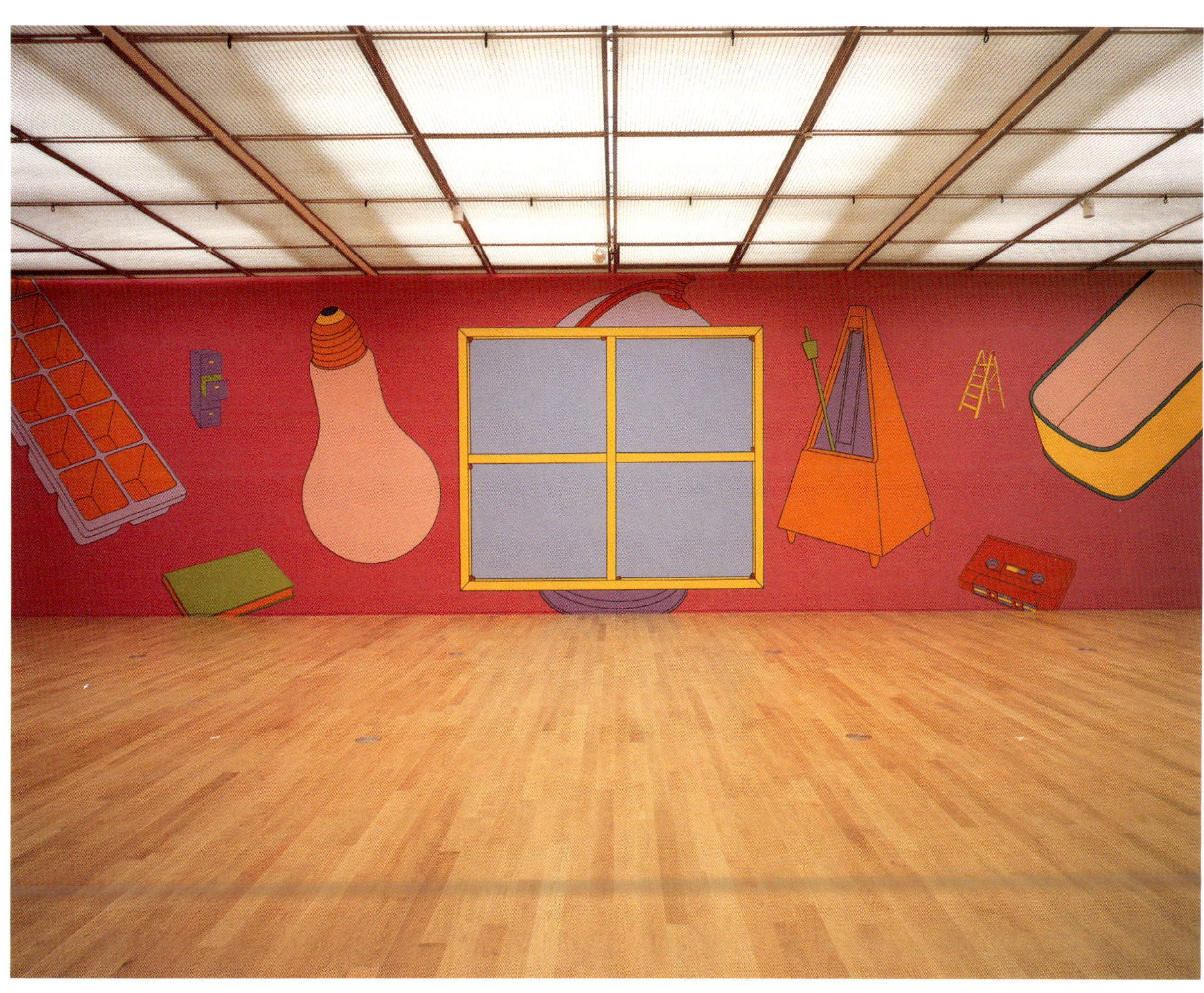

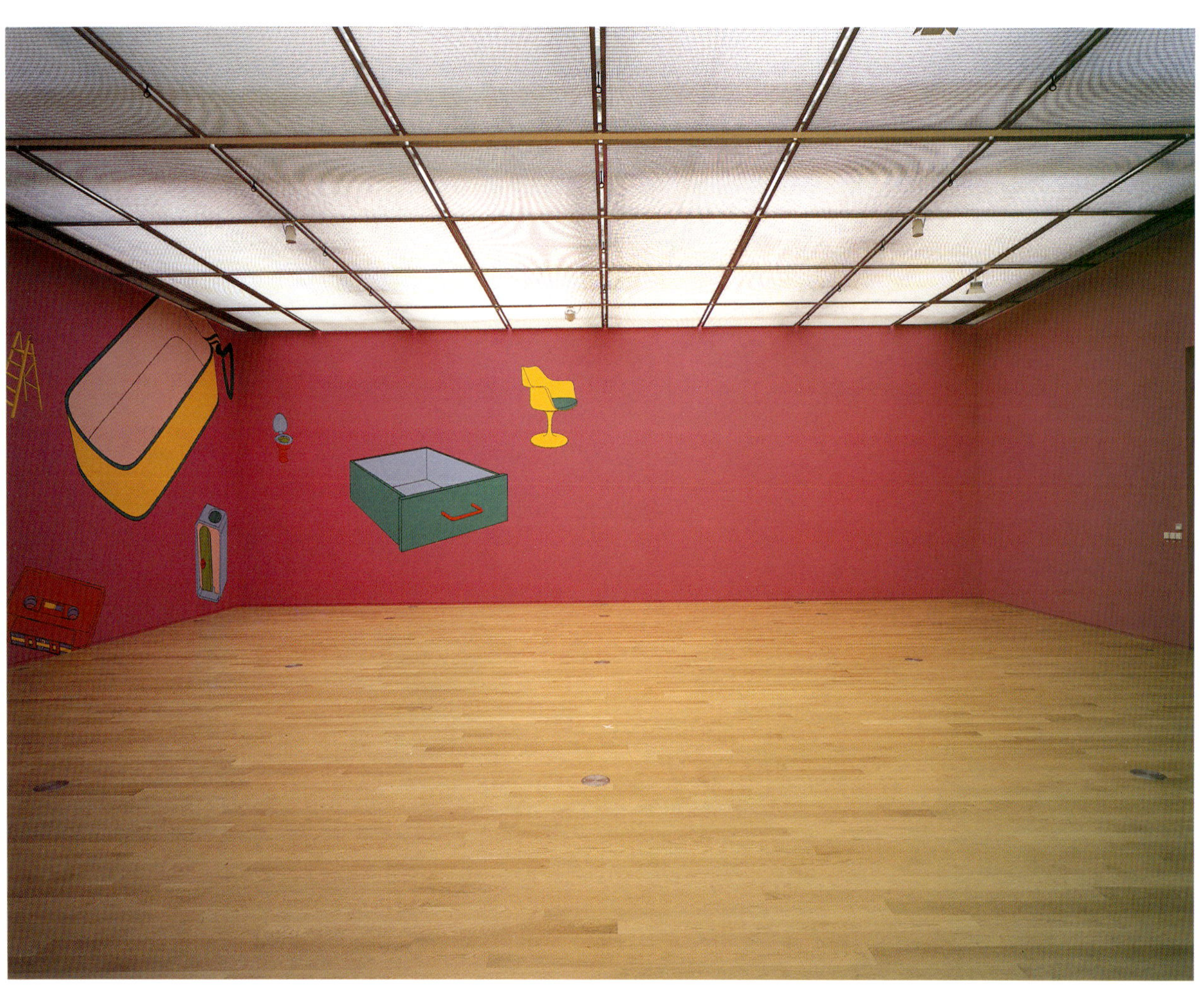

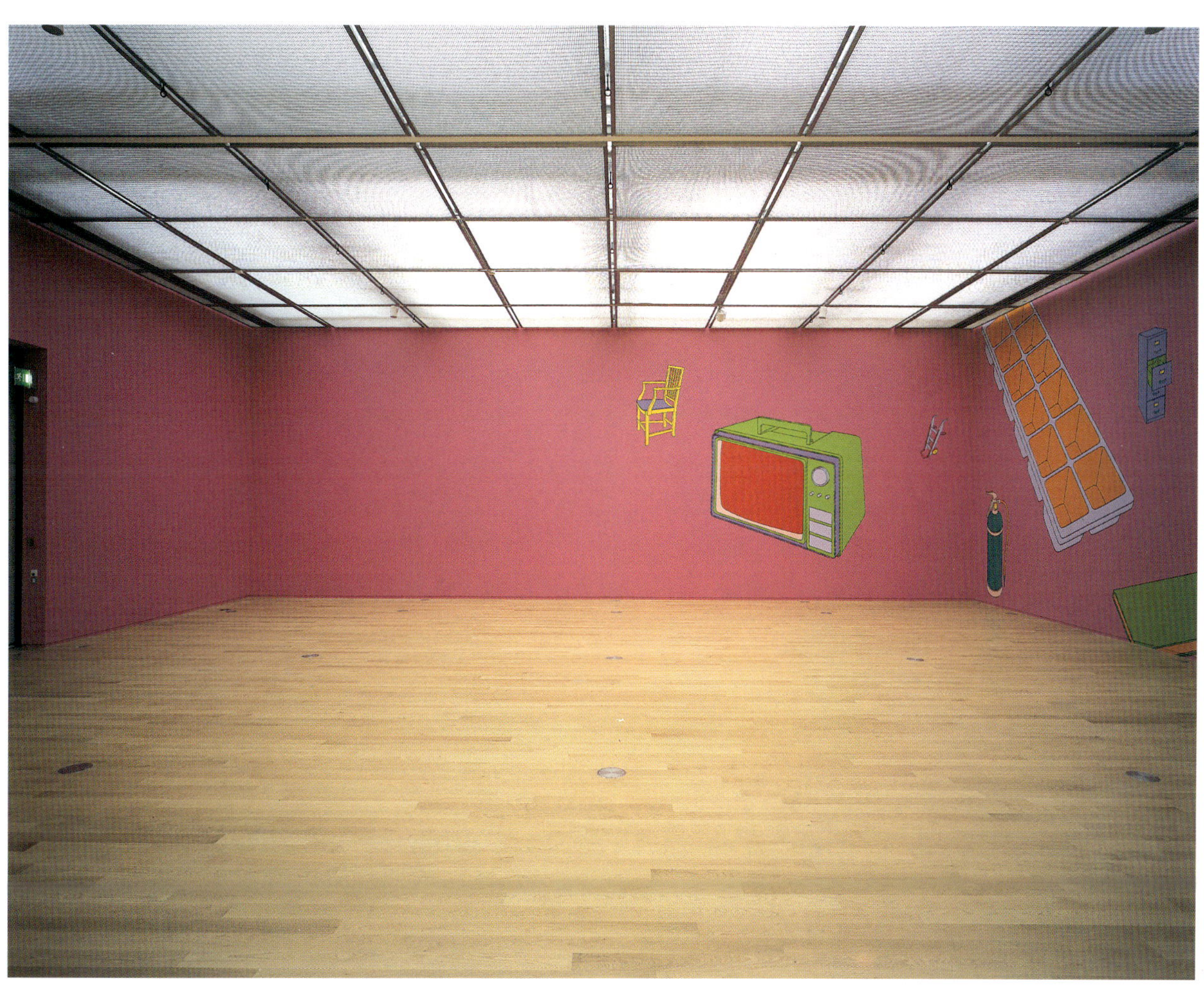

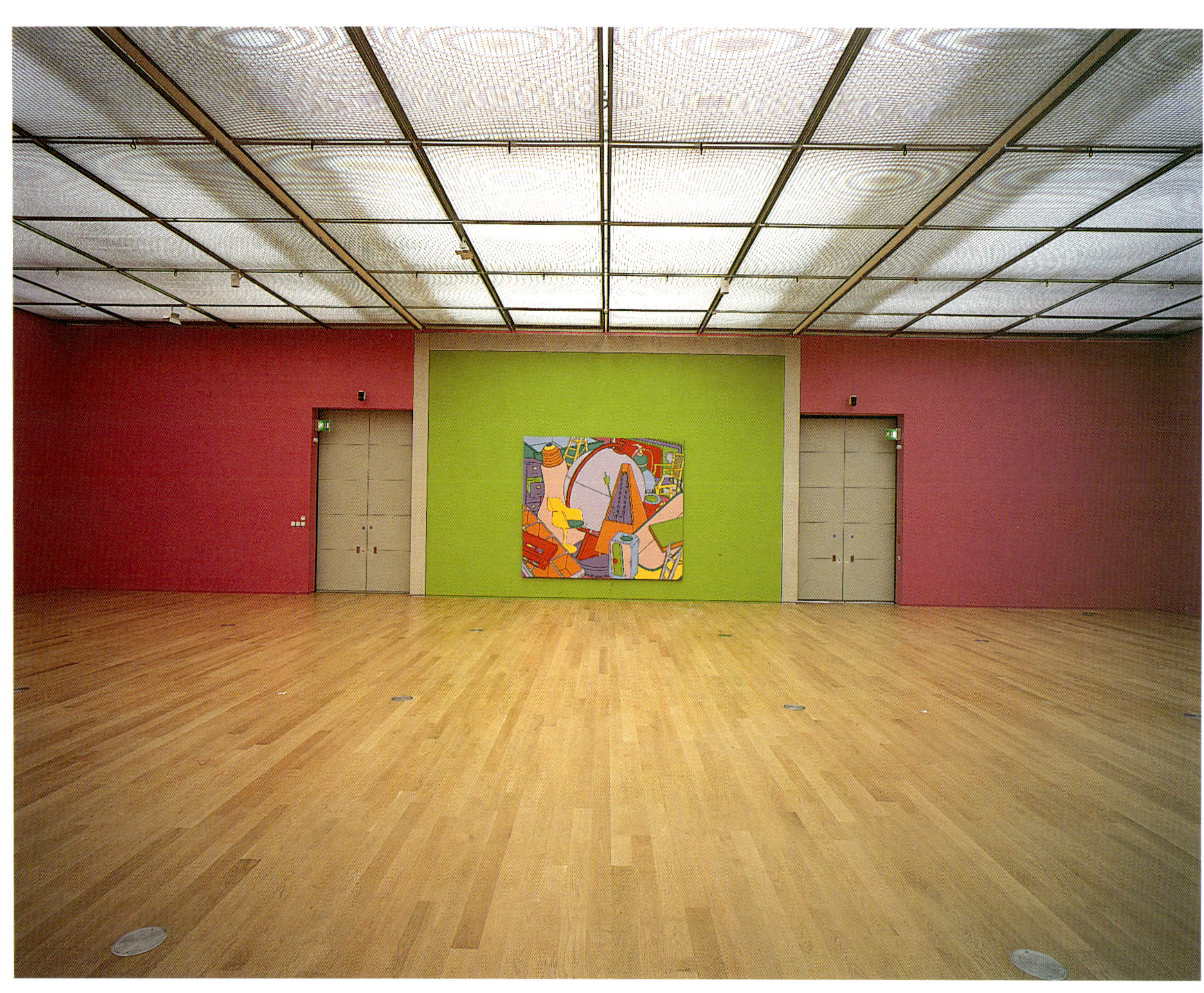

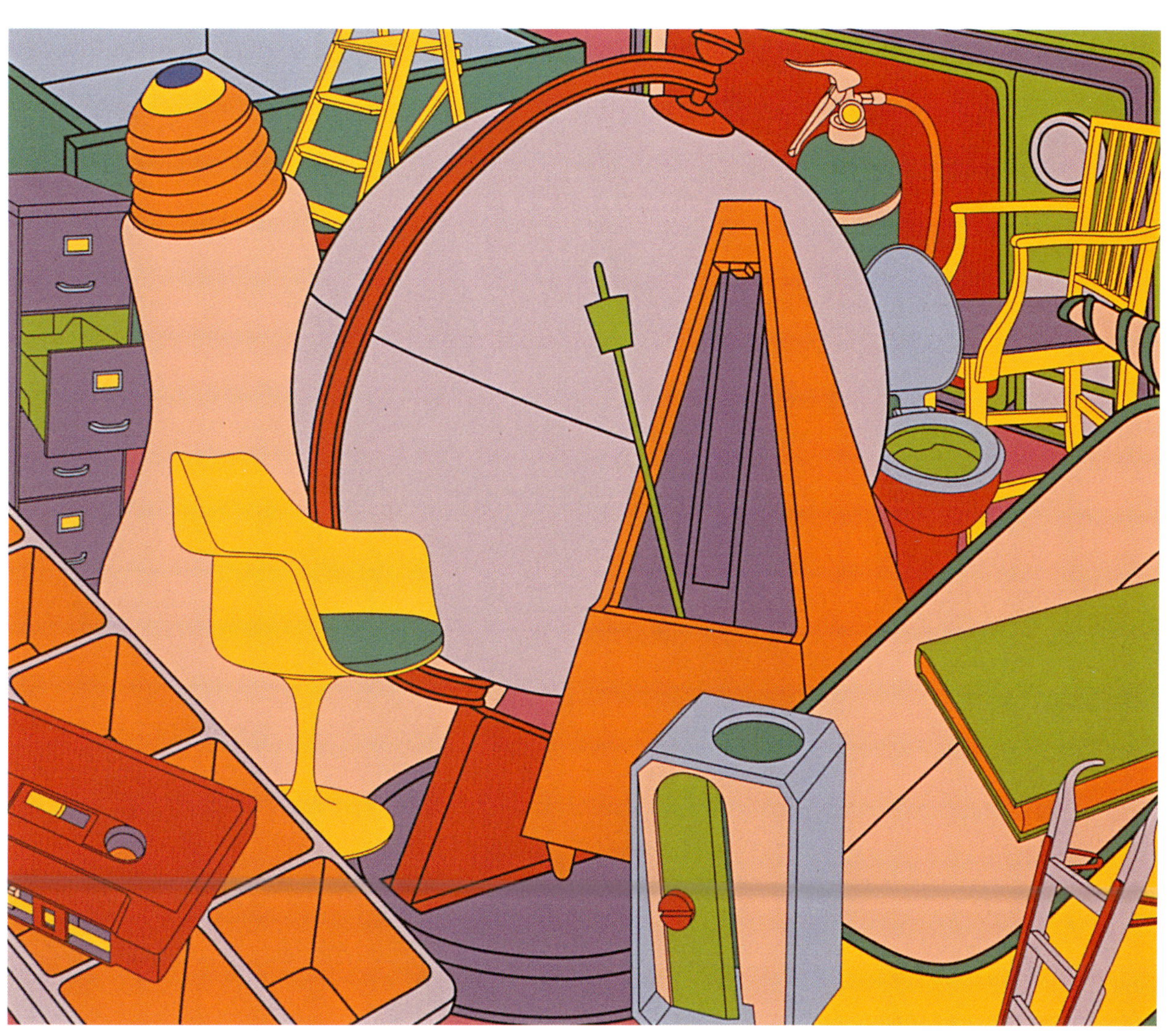

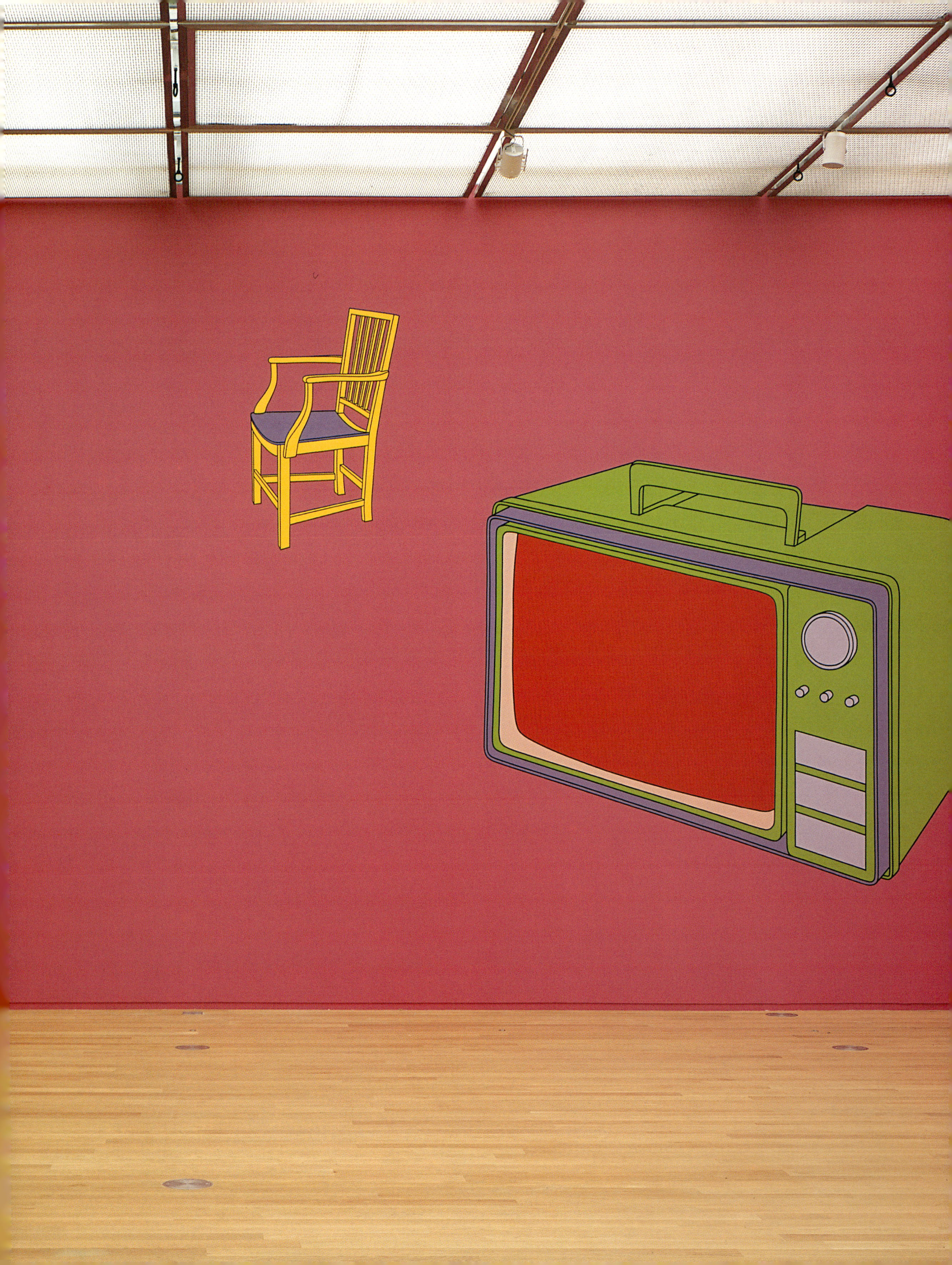

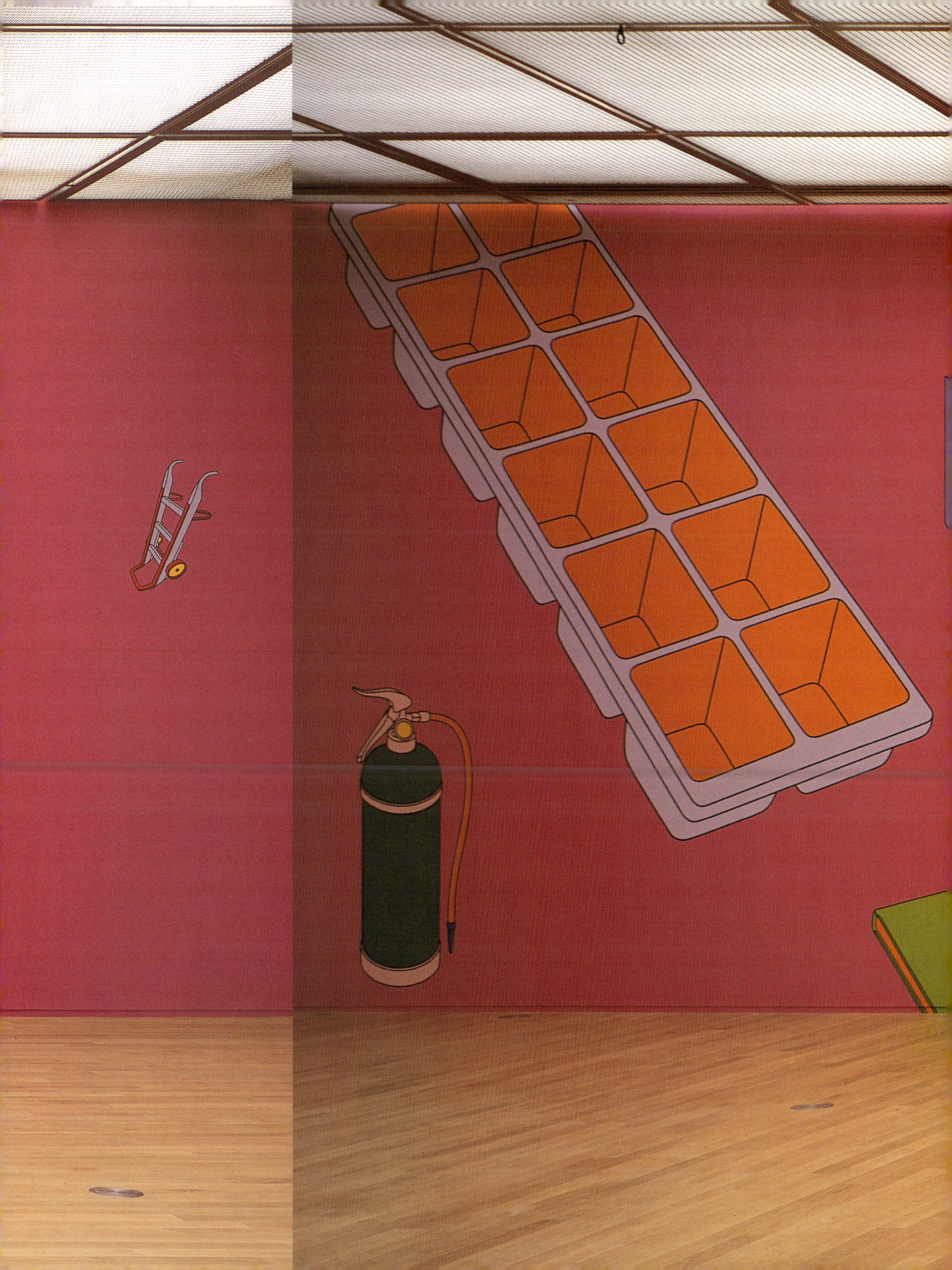

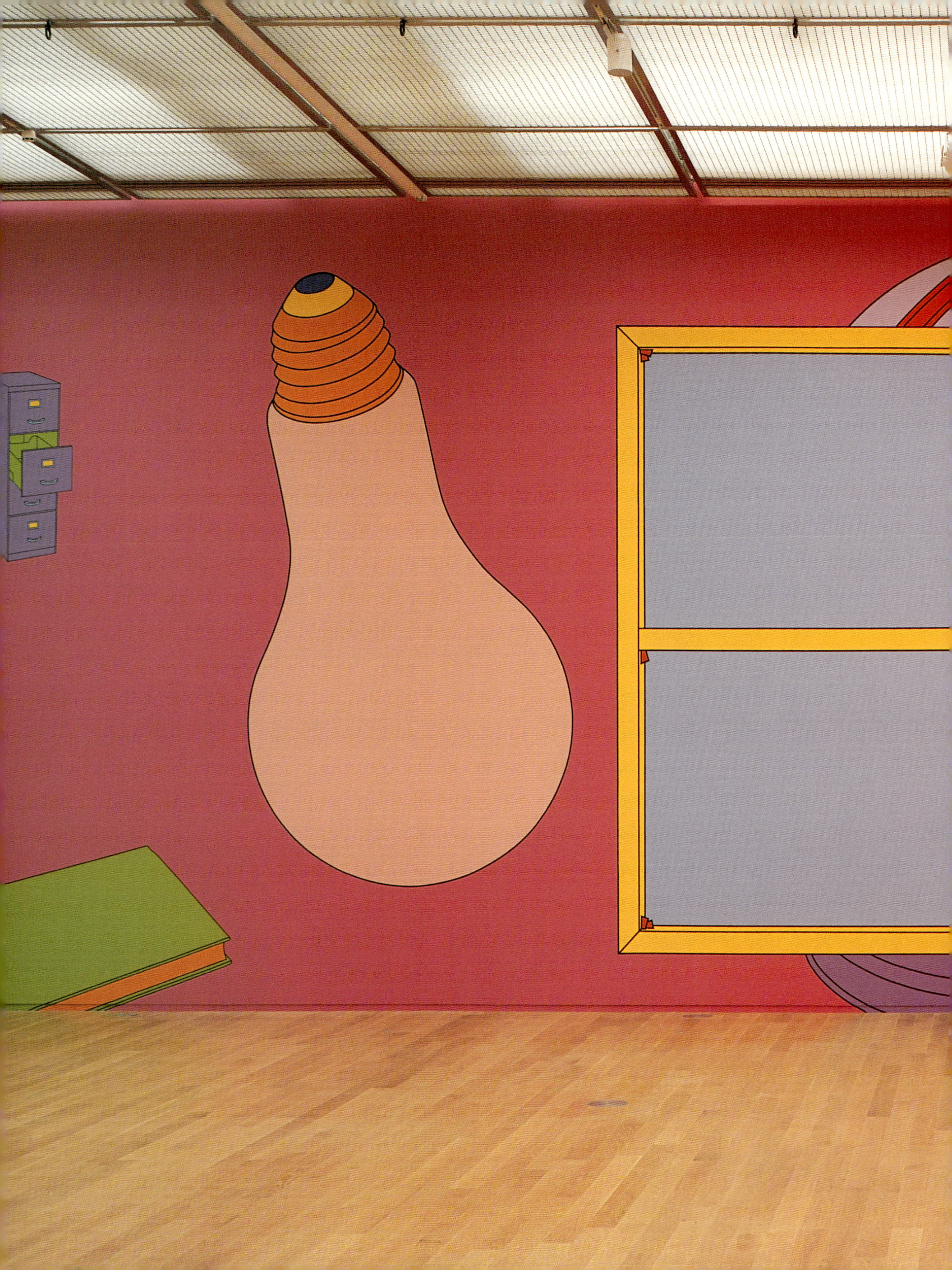

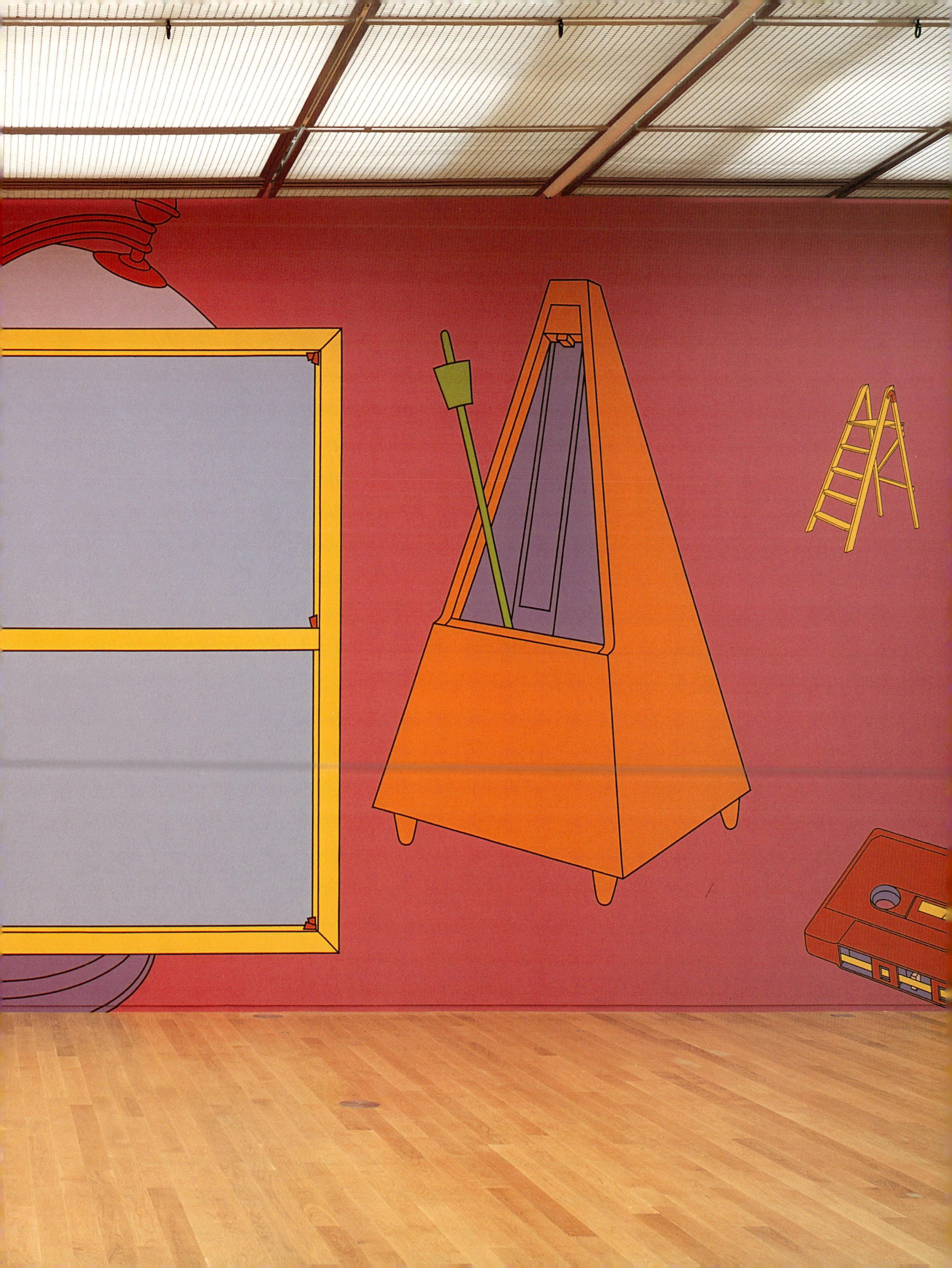

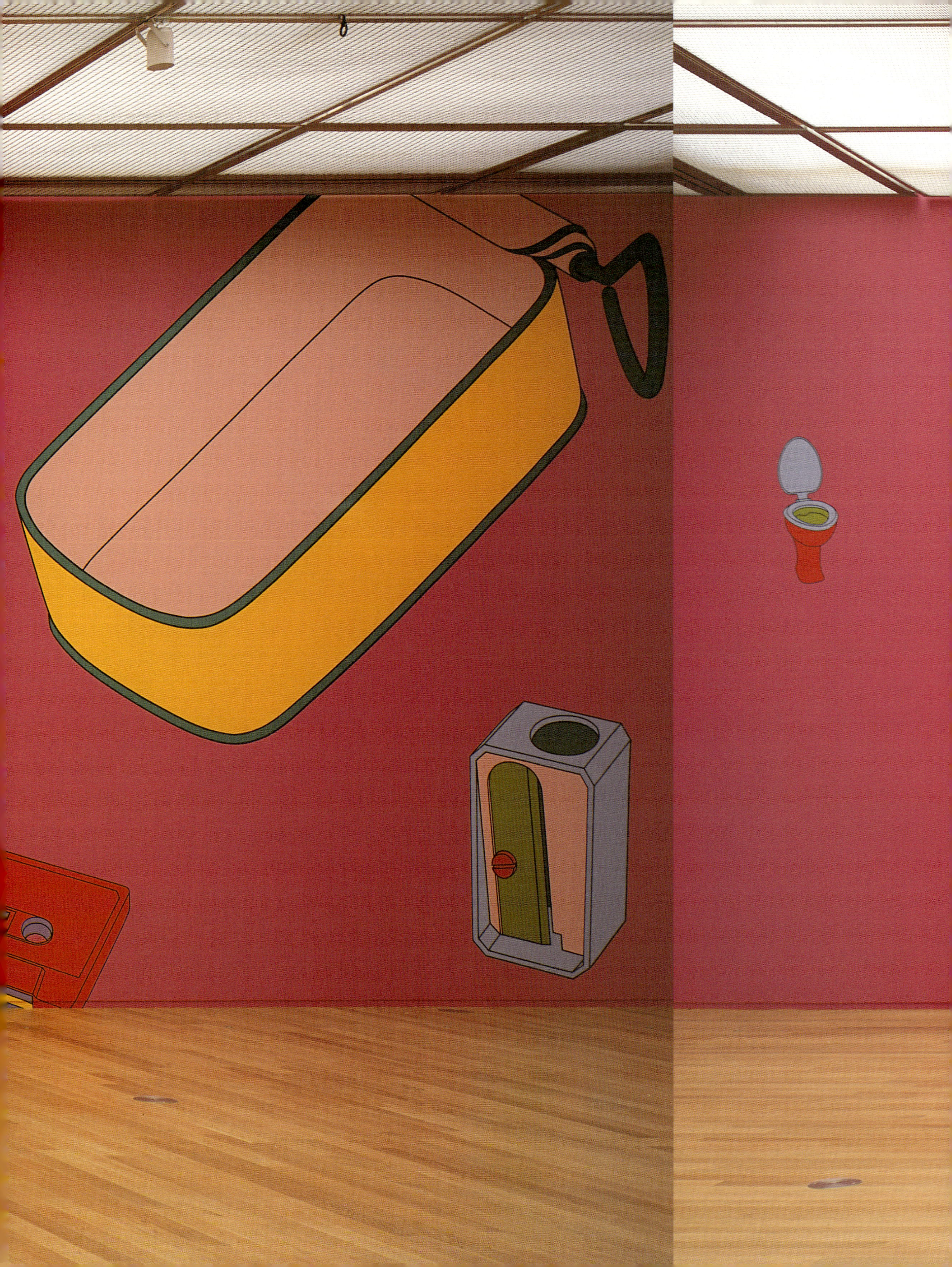

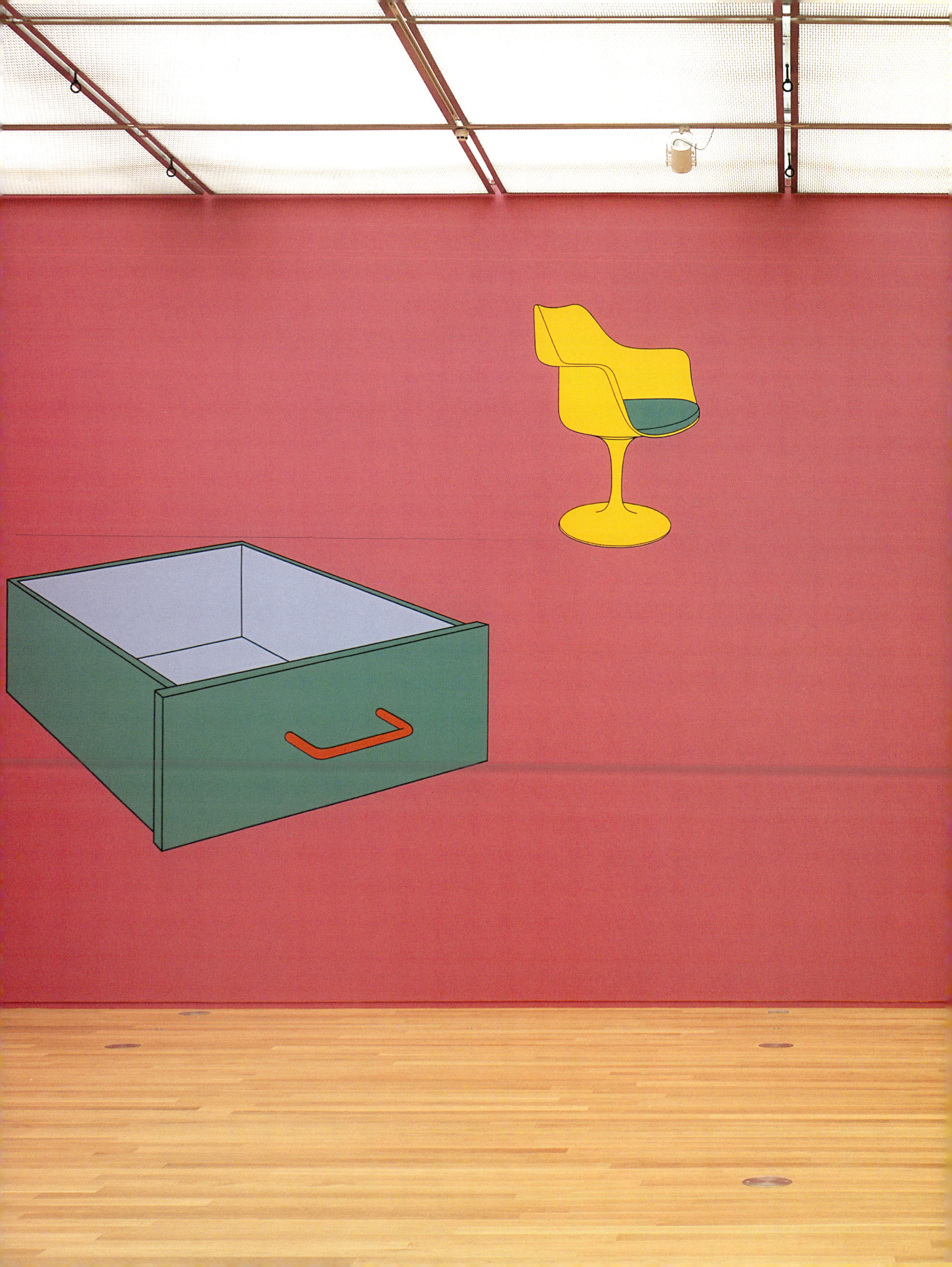

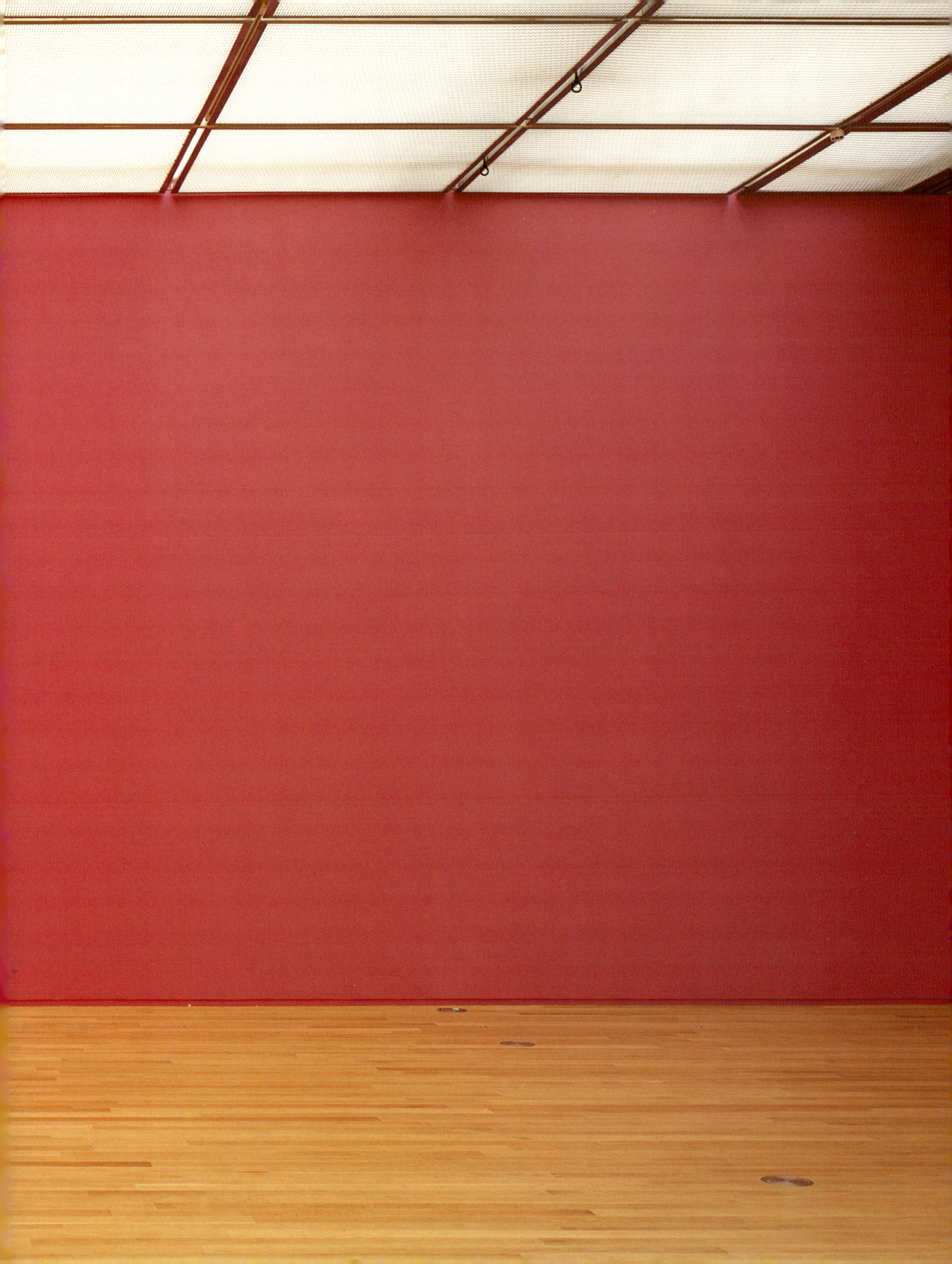

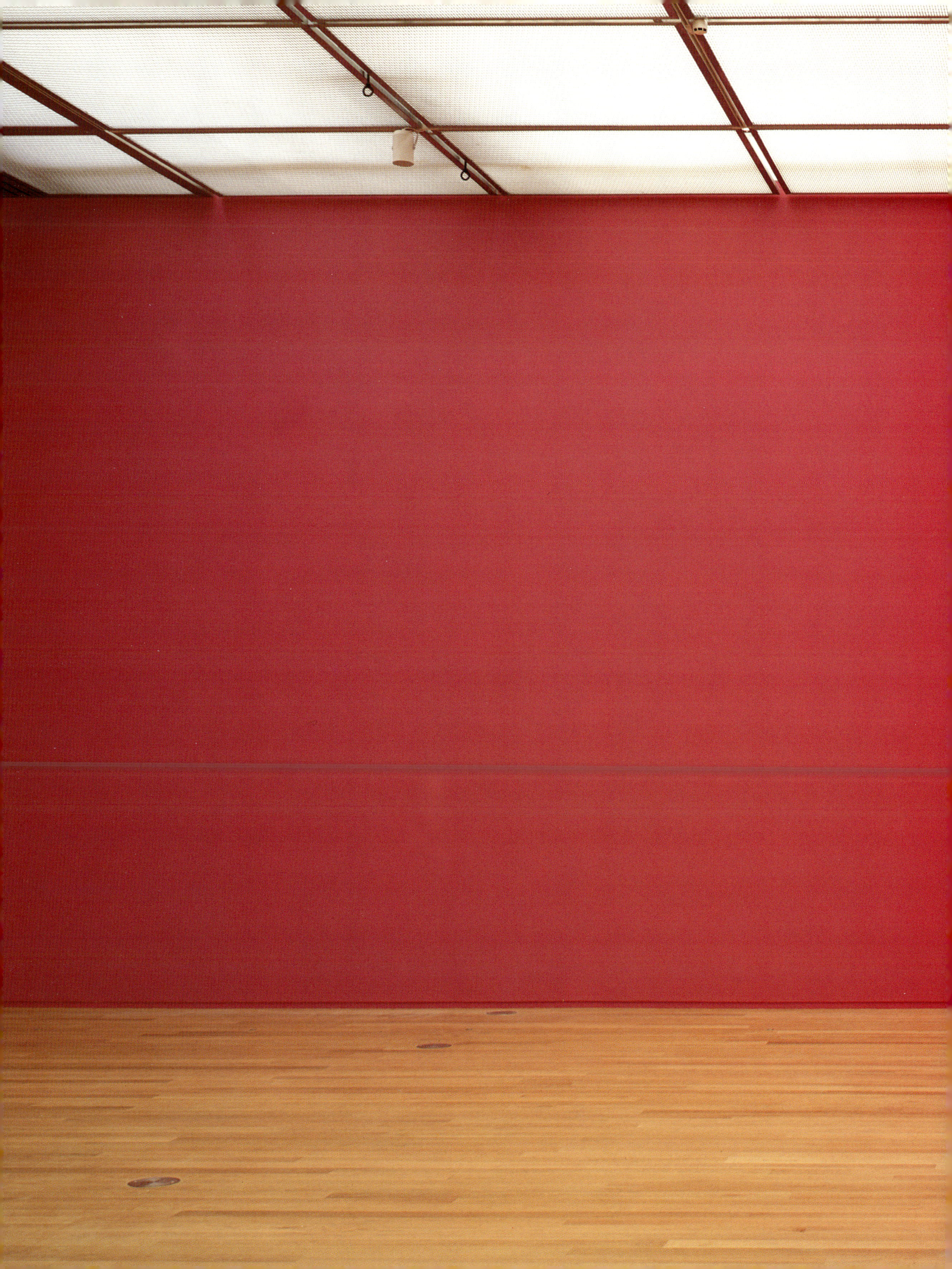

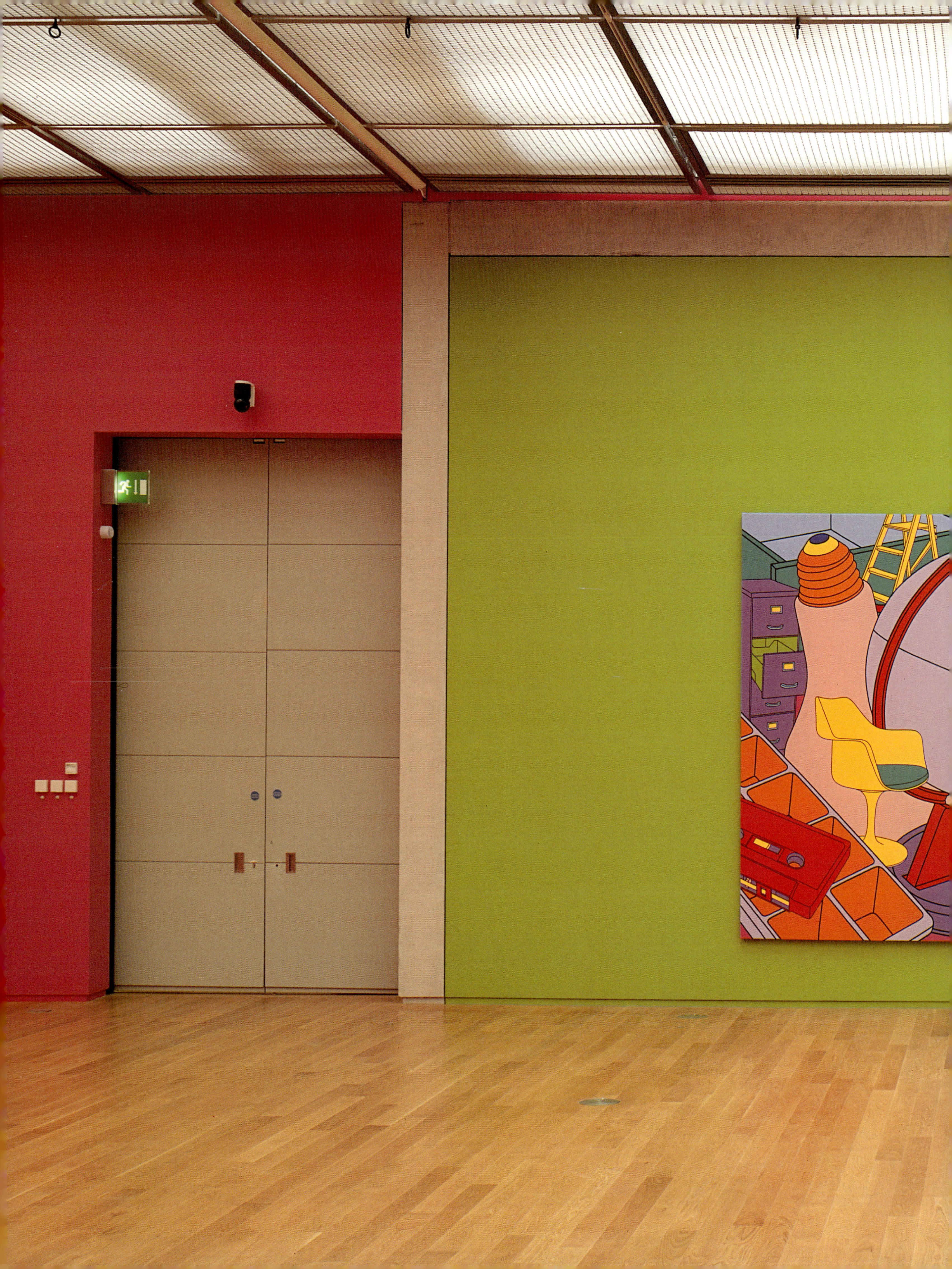

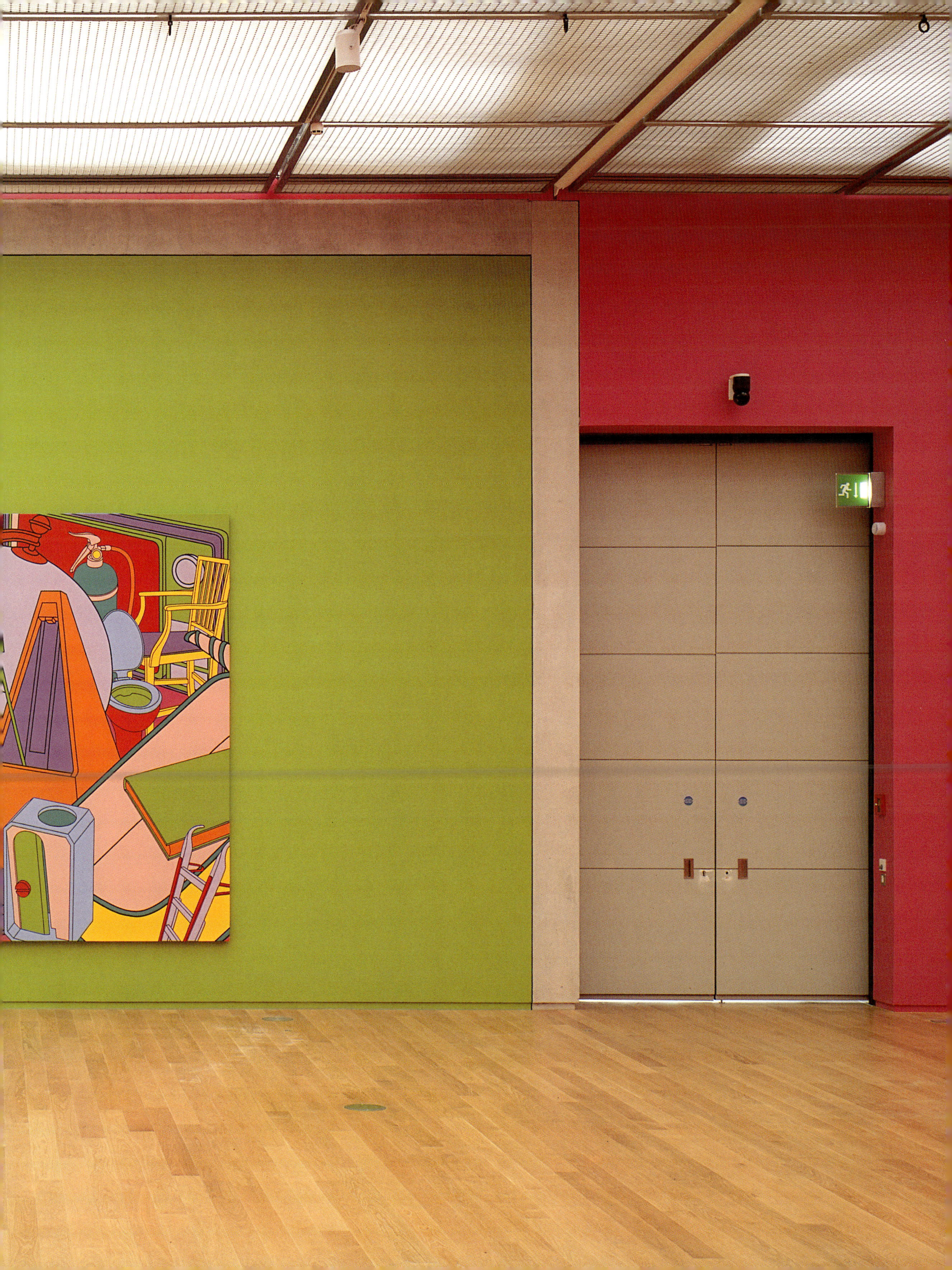

Biographical Notes

Michael Craig-Martin was born in Dublin in 1941. He grew up and was educated in the United States, studying Fine Art at the Yale University School of Art and Architecture. He moved to Britain on completion of his studies in 1966 and has lived and worked here ever since.

His first one-person exhibition was at the Rowan Gallery, London in 1969. Since that time he has exhibited in numerous solo and group exhibitions both in Britain and internationally, including the definitive exhibition of British conceptual art, The New Art, curated by Anne Seymour at the Hayward Gallery in 1972. His work has been concerned with fundamental questions about the nature of art, about represent-ation, authorship, and the role of the viewer, explored primarily through commonplace objects, both real and as images. His best known works include An oak tree of 1973, in which he claimed to have changed a glass of water into an oak tree, his large-scale wall drawings of common objects, and his recent intensely coloured room installations and paintings.

A major retrospective of his work was held in London at the Whitechapel Art Gallery in 1989. In 1995, he curated Drawing the Line, a comprehensive exhibition of line drawings from prehistory to the present day, which toured to four galleries, including the Whitechapel. He created large-scale, site-specific installations at the Kunstvereins in Düsseldorf (1997), in Hannover (1998) and in Stuttgart (1999).

He represented Great Britain at the São Paulo Bienal in 1998 and created a major wall painting installation covering the ground floor of the Museum of Modern Art, New York in 1999. During 2000 he made installations at Tate Britain, London, the Haus der Kunst, Munich, and at IVAM, Valencia. These were followed by installations at the Berardo Museum, Sintra, Portugal and the Douglas Hyde Gallery, Dublin.

He is widely recognised for his influence as a teacher at Goldsmiths College where his students included Julian Opie, Gary Hume, Sarah Lucas, Fiona Rae, Richard Patterson, and Liam Gillick. He was appointed Millard Professor of Fine Art at Goldsmiths from 1994 to 2000, and was subsequently made Professor Emeritus of Fine Art. He was a Trustee of the Tate Gallery from 1989 to 1999. In 2001 he was awarded a CBE.

His work is represented by the Gagosian Gallery.

Selected One Person Exhibitions

1969
Rowan Gallery, London (also 1970, 1972, 1973, 1974, 1975, 1976, 1978, 1980)

1971
Arnolfini Gallery, Bristol
Richard Demarco Gallery, Edinburgh

1974
Galerie December, Münster

1976-77
Michael Craig-Martin: Selected Works 1966-1975, Turnpike Gallery, Leigh; touring Britain

1977
Oliver Dowling Gallery, Dublin

1978
Galerie December, Düsseldorf
Michael Craig-Martin: 10 works 1970-77, Institute of Modern Art, Brisbane; touring Australia

1979
Galeria Foksal, Warsaw
Galeria Akumlatory, Poznan, Poland
Oliver Dowling Gallery, Dublin

1980
Galerie Bama, Paris

1981
Galerija Suvremene Umjetnosti, Zagreb

1982
Fifth Triennale India, New Delhi
Waddington Galleries, London

1985
Waddington Galleries, London

1988
Waddington Galleries, London

1989
Michael Craig-Martin: A Retrospective 1968-1989, Whitechapel Art Gallery, London

1990
Galerie Claudine Papillon, Paris

1991
Projects 27, Museum of Modern Art, New York (site specific installation)
David Nolan Gallery, New York
Musée des Beaux-Arts, André Malraux, Le Havre

1992
Waddington Galleries, London

1993
Accommodating, British School at Rome (site specific installation)
Galerie Claudine Papillon, Paris (site specific installation)
At home, Waddington Galleries, London

1994
Private space, public space, Centre Georges Pompidou, Paris (site specific installation)
Wall paintings at the Villa Herbst, Museum Sztuki, Lodz, Poland (site specific installation)
An oak tree, Galeria Foksal, Warsaw

1995
Museum of Contemporary Art, Chicago (site specific installation)

1997
Innocence and experience, Waddington Galleries, London
Michael Craig-Martin: Prints, Alan Cristea Gallery, London
Michael Craig-Martin und Raymond Pettibon, Kunstverein für die Rheinlande, Düsseldorf (site specific installation)

1998
Michael Craig Martin: Always Now, Kunstverein, Hannover (site specific installation)
British Pavilion, Ibirapuera Park, 24th International Bienal of São Paulo (site specific installation)
Mario Diacono Gallery, Boston

1999
Michael Craig-Martin: and sometimes a cigar is just a cigar, Württembergischer Kunstverein, Stuttgart (site specific installation)

Selected Group Exhibitions

ModernStarts: Things, Museum of Modern Art, New York (site specific installation)
Common History, Peter Blum Gallery, New York

2000
Conference, Waddington Galleries, London
IVAM, Valencia, Spain (site specific installation)
Full/empty. FIG-1, London

2001
Landscapes, Douglas Hyde Gallery, Dublin (site specific installation)
Living, Sintra Museum of Modern Art, Berardo Collection, Portugal

2002
Inhale/Exhale, Manchester Art Gallery (site specific installation)

1972
7 Exhibitions, Tate Gallery, London
The New Art, Hayward Gallery, London

1973
11 British Artists, Staatlichen Kunsthalle, Baden-Baden; touring to Kunsthalle, Bremen
Henry Moore to Gilbert & George, Palais des Beaux-Arts, Brussels

1974
Idea and Image in Recent Art, Art Institute of Chicago
Art as Thought Process, Serpentine Gallery, London

1975
IX Biennale des Jeunes Artistes, Paris
Contemporary British Drawings, XIII Biennal of São Paulo
Britanniasta 75, Helsingin Taidehalli, Helsinki; touring Finland

1976
Art as Thought Process, XI Biennale International d'Art, Palais d'Europe, Menton
Sydney Biennale, Art Gallery of New South Wales, Sydney

1977
Documenta VI, Kassel, West Germany
Hayward Annual: Current British Art Part II, Hayward Gallery, London

1978
The Garden, Jardin Botanique National; organised by Musées Royaux des Beaux-Arts de Belgique, Brussels

1979
Un Certain Art Anglais, Musée d'Art Moderne de la Ville de Paris; organised by ARC II and the British Council
JP II, Palais des Beaux-Arts, Brussels, in collaboration with the British Council

1980
ROSC, University College Gallery and National Gallery of Ireland, Dublin

1981
Malmoe, Konsthall, Malmö, Sweden
Construction in Process, Lodz, Polanda
British Sculpture in the 20th Century, Whitechapel Art Gallery, London

1982
Aspects of British Art Today, Metropolitan Art Museum, Tokyo; touring Japan

1983
New Art, Tate Gallery, London

1984
1965-1972 - when attitude became form, Kettle's Yard Gallery, Cambridge and Fruitmarket Gallery, Edinburgh

1986
Entre El Objeto Y La Imagen - Escultura británica contemporánea, Palacio Velázquez, Madrid; touring to Barcelona and Bilbao

1987
Vessel, Serpentine Gallery, London
Wall Works, Cornerhouse Gallery, Manchester

1988
Starlit Waters: British Sculpture, an International Art 1968-1988, Tate Gallery, Liverpool
Britannica: Trente Ans de Sculpture, Musée des Beaux-Arts, André Malraux, Le Havre; touring France and to Museum Van Hedendaagse Kunst, Antwerp
That Which Appears Is Good, That Which Is Good Appears, Tanja Grunert Gallery, Cologne

1989
Sculpture, Six Friedrich Gallery, Munich
Michael Craig-Martin, Grenville

Davey, Julian Opie, Lia Rumma Gallery, Naples

1990
The Readymade Boomerang, curated by Rene Block, Sydney Biennale, Sydney

1991
Objects for the Ideal Home: The Legacy of Pop Art, Serpentine Gallery, London

1993
Out of sight, out of mind, Lisson Gallery, London
Here and Now, Serpentine Gallery, London

1994
Wall to Wall, Serpentine Gallery, London (site specific installation)

1995
The Adventure of Painting, curated by Martin Hentschel and Raimund Stecker, Kunstverein, Düsseldorf and Kunstverein, Stuttgart (site specific installations)
Drawing the Line: reappraising drawing past and present, selected by Michael Craig-Martin, South Bank Centre National Touring Exhibition, Southampton City Art Gallery, and touring
1:1 Wandmalerei: wall drawings and wall paintings, Kunstlerwerkstat, Munich (site specific installation)

1996
Un siècle de sculpture Anglaise, Galerie Nationale du Jeu de Paume, Paris

1997
Treasure Island, Calouste Gulbenkian Foundation, Lisbon
Follow Me: British Art on the Lower Elbe, organised by Lanschaftsverband Stade, Buxtehude Museum, Germany (site specific installation)
Love Hotel, organised by National Gallery of Australia, touring Australia

Commissions

1998
Elegant Austerity, Waddington Galleries, London

Jardin d'artiste, Musée Zadkine, Paris Up to 2000, Southampton City Art Gallery
Cluster Bomb, Morrison Judd, London

2000
Live in your head, Whitechapel Art Gallery, London; touring to Museo do Chiado, Lisbon (2001)
Intelligence: New British Art 2000, Tate Britain, London (site specific installation)
Die scheinbaren Dinge, Haus de Kunst, Munich (site specific installation)
Voila, Le Monde dans la tete, Musée d'Art Moderne de la Ville de Paris, Paris
Shifting Ground, Irish Museum of Modern Art, Dublin
Drawings 2000, Barbara Gladstone Gallery, New York
Drawings & Photographs, Matthew Marks Gallery, New York

2001
Lux Gallery, London
Yale School of Art and Architecture, New Haven

2002
Passenger, Astrup Fearnley Museum, Oslo

1975
Margate District Council (neon drawing)

1983
Midland Bank, New York (painted canvas and metal reliefs)

1984
Colchester District General Hospital, Essex (wall painting)

1988
Hasbro-Bradley UK Ltd, Stockley Park, Middlesex (wall painting)

1990-91
Rosehaugh Stanhope Investments plc for Broadgate, London (large scale drawings in gold leaf on glass, two windows)

1992
Morgan-Stanley International, Canary Wharf, London (4-part circular wall drawing)
Ballet Rambert, set and costume design for Gone choreographed by MarkBaldwin, premiered at Royal Northern College of Music, Manchester

1994-95
Tokyo International Exhibition Centre, Tokyo (wall painting)

1997
Shop Fitting, Jigsaw, New Bond Street, London (temporary installation)
Mark Baldwin Dance Company, costume design for M-Piece, Queen Elizabeth Hall, London
EU Council meeting, Lancaster House, London (temporary installation)
Millennium Dome Commission, proposal for site specific sculpture

1999
ABN Amro Headquarters, Amsterdam (wall painting) (architects: I.M. Pei)
Milton Keynes Theatre and Milton Keynes Gallery (metal relief)

Thames & Hudson, Publishers, London (temporary installation)
Swiss Light, Tate Modern (collaboration with architects Herzog & deMeuron)

2000
British Embassy, Moscow (painting on canvas) (architects: Ahrends Burton)
British Council Building, Berlin (ceiling painting) (architects: Sauerbruck Hutton)
Royal Mail - design of millennium commemorative postage stamp (theme: right to health)
Glasgow Collection (Design Museum) commission to design a piece of furniture:
Sofa/bed/table/desk/shelving
Ivy Restaurant, London, design of stained glass windows and exterior clock
Museum of Modern Art, New York, digital artwork (screensaver)
Museum of Modern Art, New York, special millennium poster

2001
Landeszentralbank, Gera (wall paintings) (architects : David Chipperfield)
BBC, London, *Coloured tv*, digital artwork (screensaver)

2002
Williams-Sonoma Corporation Headquarters, San Francisco (painting on canvas)
Norddeutsche Landesbank Headquarters, Hannover (wall painting) (architects: Behnisch, Behnisch and Partner)
Laban Dance Centre, London, artist consultant to architects Herzog & deMeuron and site specific installation (large scale digitally produced image on vinyl)
Regents Place, London, large scale digitally produced image on vinyl in light box (architects: Sheppard Robson)
Modern Painters, image for magazine cover and 8 page curated section, March issue

Biographies Contributors

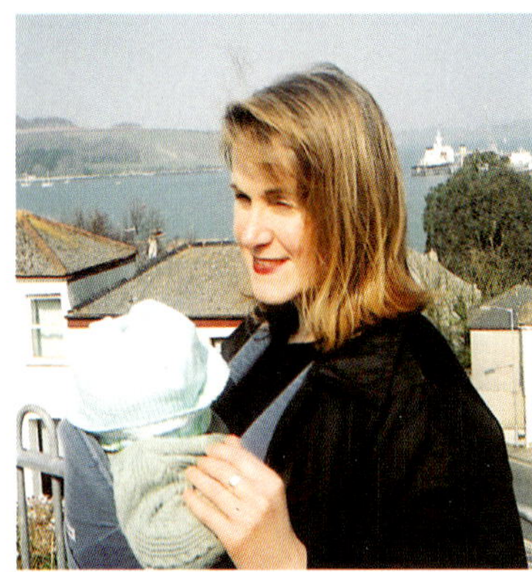

Virginia Button is a writer and curator based in Cornwall. She previously worked at the Tate Gallery for ten years, curating *The Turner Prize* (1993-98), *Art Now*, and in 2000 co-curated with Charles Esche, *Intelligence*, the first triennial of contemporary British Art at Tate Britain. She is author of *The Turner Prize* (revised ed.1999).

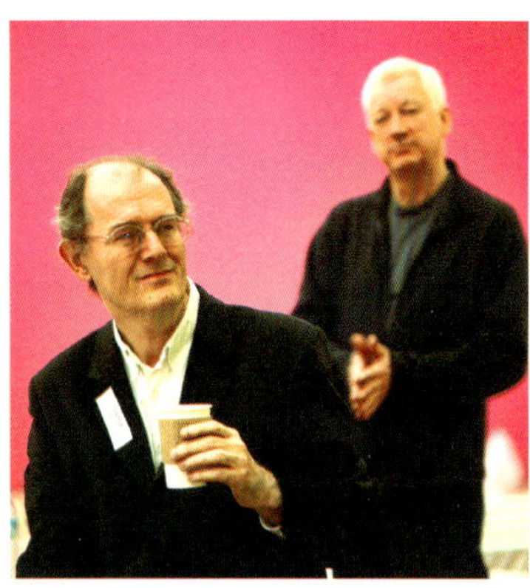

Richard Cork is an art critic, historian, broadcaster and exhibition organiser. He has been Art Critic of *The Listener*, *Evening Standard* and *The Times* and has organised major exhibitions at the Tate Gallery, the Royal Academy and elsewhere. His books include a two-volume study of *Vorticism* (1976); *Art Beyond the Gallery* (1985); and, in 2002, four volumes of his selected critical writings.

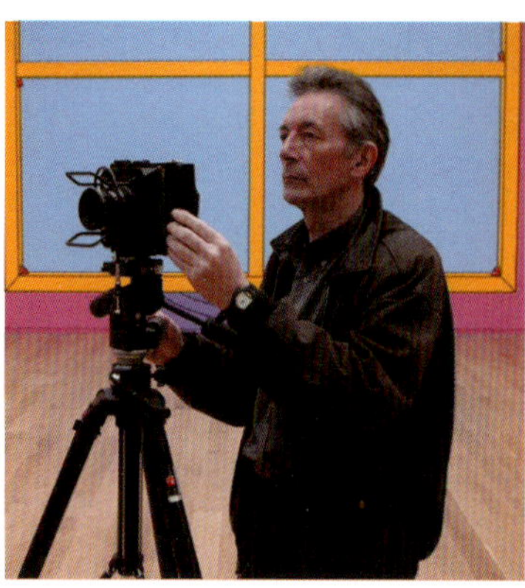

John Davies is a documentary and art photographer who has studied aspects of the urban landscape. His work is represented in various US and European collections. He is currently working on *Metropoli*, an ambitious project exploring the major industrial and post-indusrtial cities of the UK at the beginning of the new century.

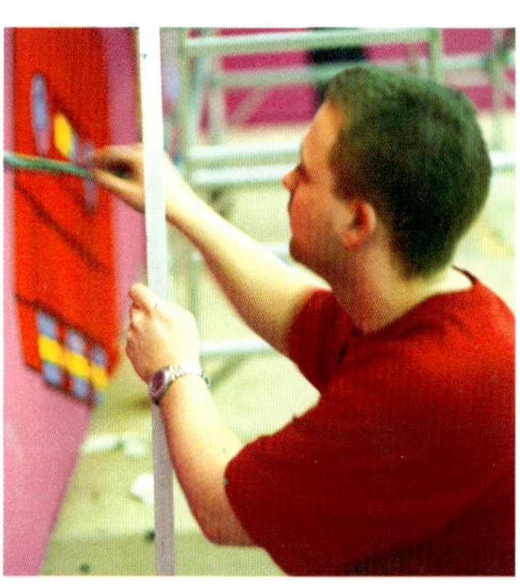

Paul Hosking studied at Goldsmiths College, London where he lives and works. His work has been selected for *Beck's Futures* 2002 at the ICA, London.

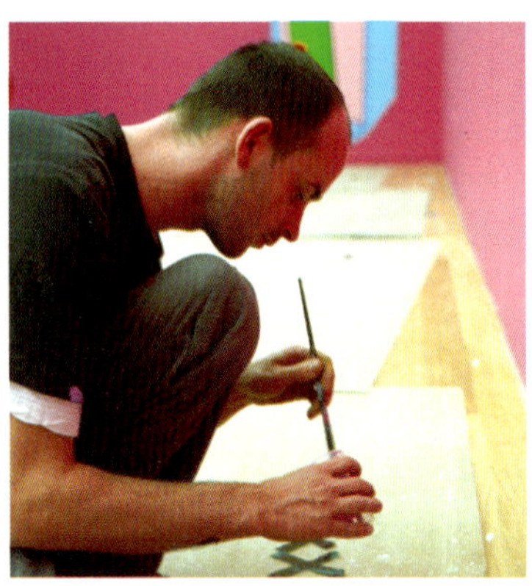

Paul Needham is an artist living and working in Manchester. He is currently studying for an MA in Fine Art at Manchester Metropolitan University. Previously, he has exhibited in Manchester, Liverpool, Amsterdam and New York.

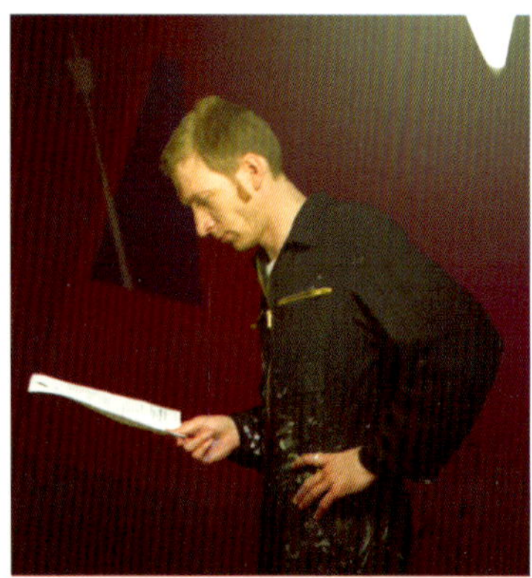

Jost Muenster was born in Ulm Germany and is currently living and working in London where he is studying for an MA in Fine Art at Goldsmiths College.

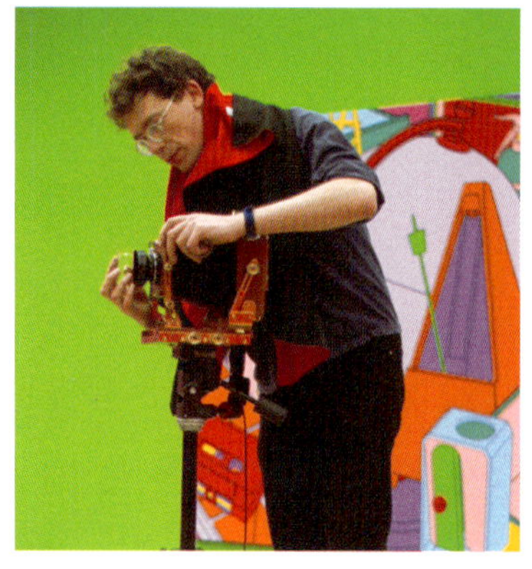

Richard Weltman is a fine art photographer living and working in Manchester. He studied at Leeds University and has worked at Viewpoint Gallery, Salford and Manchester Art Gallery. He is currently visiting lecturer at the University of Central Lancashire.

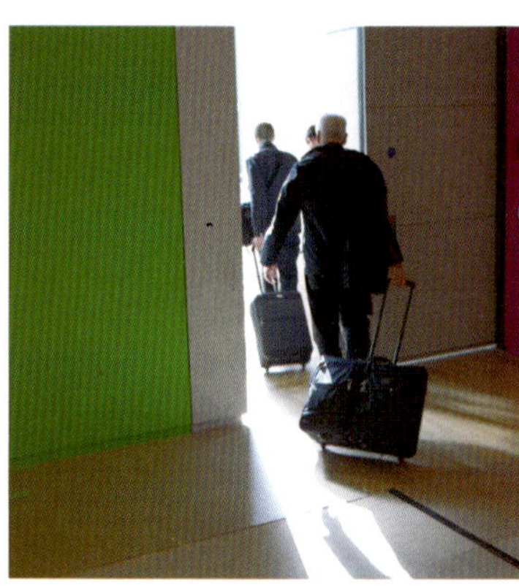

Finis